Opening Spaces

Birkhäuser – Publishers for Architecture
Basel · Berlin · Boston

Hans Loidl_Stefan Bernard

Opening Spaces
Design as Landscape Architecture

Contents

6 Talking about designs – a few introductory remarks
8 In the form of open space

[1] Form and forming
12
14 Point - line - area - solid
14 Order
16 Shape and form
17 *Coherence and prior experience*
18 Form
18 *Superization*
20 Form components
21 *Induction*
22 Forming, design
23 *Connection and landscape architecture projects*

[2] Designing and design
26
29 Between head and hand
29 Designing
31 The design
31 *Intersubjectivity*
33 Intention
33 Creativity
34 *Bifurcation*
35 *The usual design path*
36 *Working model for the design process (Darke, Lawson)*
37 Means and end
39 Prevailing conditions
40 Sign and Content

[3] Space - place - path
44
46 **3.1 Creating space ("space")**
48 Space
48 Spaces in landscape architecture
49 4 propositions for creating landscape architecture space
55 "Pure" space
56 Breaking down "pure" space
58 Suggesting space
62 Spatial sequences – spatial gradations
62 From closed to open spaces
64 Spatial boundaries
65 Uniformity of area
66 *Spatial size dependent on human proximity*
68 Space and the effect of space
70 *The human field of vision*
76 *Spatial effect and plants*
77 Creating space with height differences
80 Height differences and spatial effect
82 Planting to achieve visual changes of relief
85 The grove
90 **3.2 Creating focal points ("place")**
91 Focal point
94 Special position
96 *The straight line and the right angle*
97 Emphasized (designed) focal points

3.3 Movement and access ("path")	102	
Movement – motive and reaction	103	
Anticipatory orientation	103	
Proceeding "inattentively"	104	
"Beaten" track – the archetypal path	109	
Positive control	110	
External and internal access	111	
Problems/aims of internal access	111	
Path and goal	114	
Path routing and visual links	118	
Path signs and markers	120	
Trees as path markers	122	
Colonnades and arcades	124	
Path joints	126	
The seat (or bench) – a (stopping) behaviour archetype	132	
Network of paths	134	
Path routing and use of the area	134	
Path routing and spatial shapes	136	
Paths and spatial sequences	140	
	144	**[4] Design qualities**
4.1 Fundamentals of good design	146	
Form and coherence	147	
Uniformity through common features	147	
Shared position	148	
Common features in terms of appearance	150	
Theoretical/thematic common features	150	
Diversity	152	
Satisfying variety – the disturbance of uniformity	154	
4.2 Characteristics of good design	158	
Stimulation/uncertainty	159	
Tension	161	
Weight/balance	164	
Harmony	165	
Linking idea/theme/concept	166	
Clarity	168	
Simplicity	168	
4.3 Repetition as a tool	172	
Repetition	173	
Structure	176	
Patterns	176	
Grids	177	
Variation	178	
Transformation	179	
Rhythm	181	
Proportion	181	
Scale	182	
Symbols	183	
Literature	188	
Authors	190	

Talking about design – a few introductory remarks

Can one (two?) talk about designs and exchange ideas about their qualities and defects in words, or would it be better to take as many designs as possible and show how they came into being (preliminary sketches, formal "building bricks")? Can there be any way of verbalizing design that is more than just a colloquial version of something that the design itself says much more clearly and unambiguously?

And then another thing: what are we supposed to measure this sort of discussion against – if we think it is possible to have it at all? Are we not all too well aware that designs are largely ambivalent, imprisoned in a mass of detail or necessarily imprecise, or that essential information for realizing the concept is kept from the viewer?

Any attempt at analysis rapidly changes designs into a dead construct. Wouldn't it be better for absolutely all of us to get away from that as quickly as we can, and move on to the living work, or at least to images that are as close to reality as possible, and to talking about concrete things rather than drawn abstracts?

We know that historically we have always talked about design, and we still do today – in juries and professional magazines, at presentations or in the design groups themselves – and this definitely suggests that a viable link between word and design might emerge.

One reason could be that sign language and word language are coded very differently. So translation (both ways) seems helpful and necessary: it allows us to distinguish a subsequent reality from "seduction" by the design presentation. We can use language as an effective corrective to blurring and deception by colours and graphic games, resisting moving images and "beautiful pictures".

That would be an "enlightened" argument. It is of course not enough.

The second reason also lies in the coding. The pressure to translate from a graphic sign into a linguistic sign, from images into words, always represents a thrust towards abstraction, a linguistic reduction to what is essential in the image. This verbal transformation "automatically" makes principles clearer, or happens across them for the first time, shows themes and reveals connections. If we don't (can't) talk about designs, we are missing a chance to evaluate designs that is as simple as it is important. Movement in the opposite direction, translating linguistic abstractions into their pictorial equivalents, for example (pictograms), is just as important, and one of the most difficult and debilitating activities in the whole process of conveying design (anyone who has agonized painfully and endlessly over the correct way to represent a principle that is already perfectly clear from discussion will be all too aware of that).

The third reason – and an important one for this book – plops down from the tree of the above arguments like a ripe plum: I can only talk meaningfully and productively about something if the people I am talking to "speak the same language", understand me and I them, i.e. if the semantics of my word/concept are largely the same as the other's. And that is the snag: something that is taken for granted, indeed often constitutive, in the exact sciences, i.e. a fundamental understanding of certain concepts, (unfortunately?) does not apply to landscape architecture, architecture and similar creative disciplines. Here a conceptual Babel prevails, and putting your head over the design "description" parapet gets a little risky.
And for as long as we do not understand (to some extent) what we want to say to each other, talking to each other about design is an idle game (but still one that is often played).
If we can't talk about it, can't identify qualities and deficiencies precisely, then an important chance to improve things is being missed [1].
So this book attempts – or rather is compelled – to use more precise concepts about design and its content, components and qualities. We hope that this will make the content itself intelligible, and could perhaps help to cut the linguistic Babel of landscape architecture down a little.

[Hans Loidl, June 2002]

[1] "One should always say what one sees. And above all – and this is even more difficult – one should always see what one sees." (Le Corbusier)

"In the form of open space"

At a medical conference in 1837, a French doctor called Marc Dax delivered a paper about his work with aphasia [1] sufferers. He had observed that these patients had damage to the left half of the brain, whereas the right half seemed to be uninjured. Dax concluded from this that the two halves of our brains control different functions, and that the left hemisphere is responsible for our ability to speak.

Dax's ideas were not accepted at the time, but now the "hemisphere" theory is one of the foundations of modern brain research: it postulates that human perception and information processing are based on interaction between the intuitive right half of the brain, which specializes in rapid recognition and comprehension of connections, of form and space, and the logical (verbal) left half, which operates analytically and sequentially (linearly).

These insights are crucially important for this publication, which deals with design, with forming (landscape architecture objects): the perception of form (in other words the perception of landscape, space or nature as well) is a right-hemisphere action: our brain abstracts [2] large numbers of the individual pieces of information that impinge on us to make them "simple", manageable and coherent – a gestalt.

A sobering thought for all designers: in fact whatever designers dream up and realize affects the formal perception of landscape architecture objects only to a limited extent: (a number of other parameters, situative variables that the designer can scarcely influence, have their own very definite parts to play. These include the weather (rain, sun, dark clouds, broken cloud, heat, cold, storm, light breezes etc.), the seasons, the time of day (the incredible interplay of colours at sunrise, hard shadows at midday, the softness of twilight etc.), the number of other users (the happy school class on the main pathway, the couple on the edge of the wood etc.) but also the robin singing in the bushes or the rumbustious drunk on the adjacent bench. This list

[1] Aphasia: an inability to speak or understand speech as a result of brain injury. Difficulty with processing right-hemisphere, intuitively grasped material in the left hemisphere, logically.

[2] Abstraction in the sense of reducing diversity: cutting out (detailed) information with the aim of seeing essentials (more clearly).

could be continued ad infinitum. All these parameters are "simply there", are permanent and more or less simultaneously effective, but just in different forms, relating to each other at different force levels. Objects in landscape architecture simply have to let these parameters "go over their heads", "put up with them", sometimes "suffer them". But often it is precisely these unpredictable elements that can create moments of intense harmony in their interplay with a designed landscape.

Perceiving form (in landscape architecture) – a right-hemisphere experience – is thus always more, and always more complex, than the things the designer really can affect. So what does the landscape architect actually do as a designer? The – admittedly materialistic – answer has to be: landscape architects distribute solid items within an area that is being worked on topographically and structurally; they design starting-points, signs, with the aim of (gently) leading and accompanying users to create form (or space).

Given the complex way in which form is perceived, we have restricted ourselves in this book to the "feasible", to what the left hemisphere can manage to say. Above all, we have reduced the phenomenon of "landscape architecture" to make it "tangible", "comprehensible", in other words morphological.

We hope that it will be possible to discern this.

[Stefan Bernard, April 2003]

To find you in the infinite, must distinguish, then unite.

J.W. Goethe

[1] Form and forming

Forming – creating, designing – is a search for form. Form means coherence, unity. Forming means reacting to connections, and creating them. We 👥 are ways in the middle. Without us there would be no forming process and no form. That is why this first section deals with the phenomenon of form and how people perceive it. We will show how our mind makes a —— into a 🐎, and why shape can become form. We will see that we seldom see what we think we see 🚬 and why form is the mental result of our subjective prior experience. We will show that we always see a 🔪 as a ▬ , even if it looks different. And finally we will say what all that has to do with open space and how form is imposed upon it.

▬ Point - line - area - solid

The ▬**point** has no dimensions and is non-directional; it has no spatial extent, so people can't imagine or represent it. Points can only be approximated by small round areas in drawings. The ▬**line**, as a one-dimensional phenomenon, is a further development of the point, a directional sequence of points , as it were. This means that the line too is an idea [1] we cannot imagine. For an approximative representation we show it as a longitudinal area . The ▬**area** exists in two dimensions. This too exists only as an idea, as any area, however thin, will have a certain thickness, in other words an extent in the third dimension (and thus becomes a solid). In drawing, areas can be represented by outlines and/or by the content of the area . We can use point structures (**textures**) , sequences of lines (**structures**) or **colours** to represent the content of an area. ▬**Solids** are three-dimensional and thus form the "real" components of the world around us, which we perceive with our senses. Even so, if they are to be drawn we have to go back to ways used for representing the 1st and 2nd dimensions (point, line, area).

[1] Ideas, in Plato's sense, are phenomena that exist in our consciousness, even though they have never been recorded by our senses (our prior experience).

▬ Order

If a solid is represented in a drawing by its outlines , we see it [2] as three-dimensional, corporeal. If a solid is represented by its surface (e.g. by hatching) , in order to understand it ("Aha, a solid") we need several different orders or arrangements for the chosen structure . The term **order** means regularly juxtaposed (ordered) individual items (here: lines). The line itself is again the ordering concept (the context) for the regular sequence of points (see above). An area is the ordering concept for the two-dimensional arrangement of several enclosing individual lines (outlines) ; it can also be the context for one or several structures (linear structure) . Here the theoretical line joining the end points forms the outline of the area.

[2] Given the appropriate prior experience in seeing (cf. p.17, 19: context and prior experience).

Structures (linear structures) and textures (point structures) create a two-dimensional effect because of the way they are ordered. The more alike and uniform they are, the more clearly they stand out from their surroundings as a coherent entity, the more precisely the outline shape stands out from the area, the more clearly we are aware of its independence in the context.

> *Areas created by structures and textures*

Simultaneous representation of solids or areas by outlines (contour) and area character (structure, texture, colour) is not usually to be recommended. But if it has to be done: the more weakly an area is defined by its outline the clearer (more unified in contrast to the surroundings) the content of the area should be. And vice versa.

 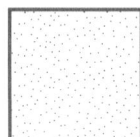     

▬ Shape and form

Outlines, structures, textures, colours and differences in brightness are the (limited) devices at our disposal for representing areas and solids by drawing; equally they are the prerequisite for our ability to see [3] solids, in other words the whole of the three-dimensional world that surrounds us, at all.

[3] What we "see" is a two-dimensional image on our retina of the three- dimensional world.

But for the complex requirements of human existence it is not enough simply to recognize solids; we have to be able to distinguish different types of solid from each other. For this reason we "give" them form by summing up different solids as units, so that we can recognize our surroundings more quickly. In this way, form is a term for typical arrangements of different qualities that make it possible – on the basis of our prior experience – for us to distinguish between visible characteristic-structures (solids) by seeing characteristic combinations of such qualities together as large entities. We call such structures made up of individual visual formations **form**. They are typical of our experience and clearly stand out from their surroundings (context).

The terms shape and form can be used analogously for (two-dimensional) line structures. But for solids "shape" is a step that leads to "form": their (out-)lines make up shapes that can be summed up as forms.

> *Coherence and prior experience*

The search for connections, for characteristic units, is an essential part of our view of the world around us. It happens every fraction of a second, with every glance. We work on a number of individual pieces of information and sensory impressions, constantly and "automatically" searching for units that we recognize because of our prior experience and as a rule can name as well (window, house, clouds, ladder etc.). At any moment, any given number of signs could be combined to create an enormous number of different connections (forms); but we instantly opt for the most probable form, and that is the one we have experienced most frequently in a particular context. The pregnance principle developed in gestalt psychology (or the law of good gestalt, or form) states that of all the possibilities for putting the parts of a whole together, that one is preferred that produces the most familiar and clearest gestalt.

Gestalt, form, means creating or working out contexts. It is based (consciously or unconsciously) on models: perceiving gestalt, being aware of form, is not chance: it is bias, or prejudice.

> *A line, an area, a shape. A unit. A form?*

▄ Form

By "giving" form we reduce the enormous number of individual pieces of information in our field of vision and thus have "our

[4] Giving form is like giving a name. | minds clear" to absorb additional information [4].

> Superization

Information aesthetics defines bundling a quantity (a "heap") of individual pieces of information together to create a context of meaning (gestalt) as "superizing individual signs to make a super-sign". The point of this mental process is that our brain has a very limited, conscious ability to absorb things; it is only by reducing the quantity of information by superizing (forming, giving gestalt) that we are able to process additional information that is already present in the perceived set of signs. This "weakness" of our brain was the cradle of thinking.

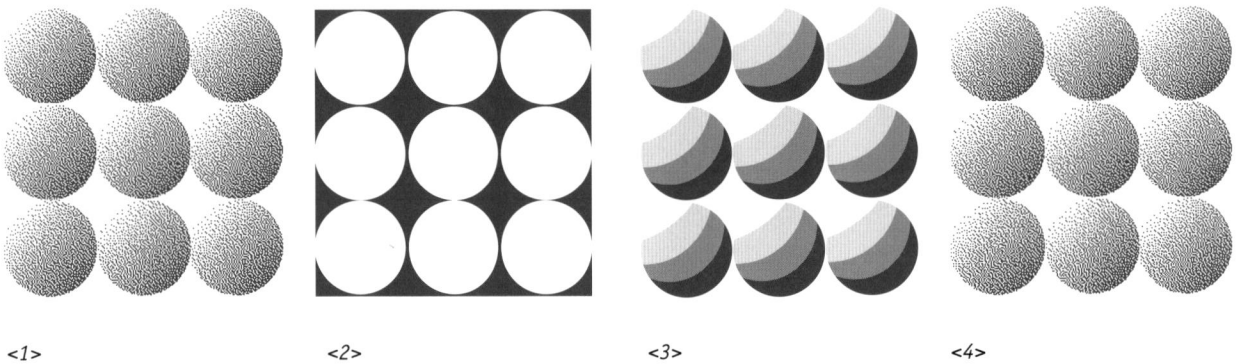

<1>   *<2>*   *<3>*   *<4>*

Texture <1> can be summed up as units (areas) in a whole variety of ways. Images <2> and <3> show summing-up devices that reduce the variety of information only a little, or only contain formal characteristics of limited familiarity. Landscape architects have prior experience of ground plan representation, so they "automatically" see nine trees of equal size with shadows, in other words units (forms) of a very typical order. Reducing the mass of information to the form "tree" makes it possible to *focus on other possible information: the trees are arranged on a strict grid, so we are dealing with an austere copse, or grove. The entire "heap of points", the various possible forms (because possible common features are contained in the point structures) have been brought together in a single form: superizing the individual signs has created a super-sign (grove of trees).*

Perceiving form means summing up (superizing) individual visual pieces of information by using our prior experience. It always relates to subjectively "knowing already", to history and stories. If we have absorbed a form (stored away an "inner picture" of it, as it were), we will always go back to this image first of all, before we look for other, less familiar interpretation possibilities. We can't do anything else.

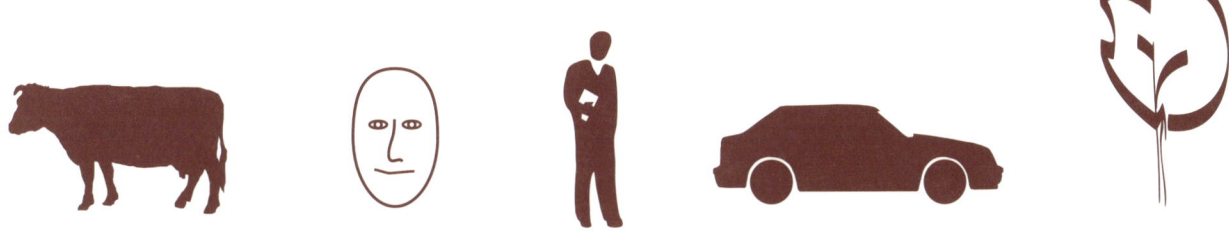

The mental transition from shape to form is not limited to "simple" contexts (a ball, a table, a car etc.), it also determines our perception of form in more complex contexts. Thus the shore-shape of a stretch of water produces lake-form, cut-out hill-shapes produce hill-form, characteristic vegetation and the shape of the site produce the "wet biotope" form.

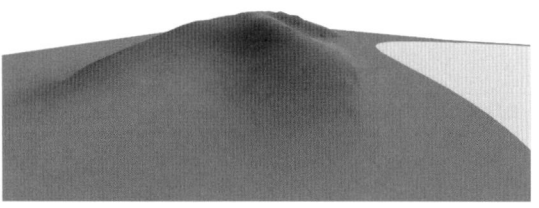

> Hill and lake

> Hill

Form components

We call partial units within a form form components. They can only be identified as such if we are already familiar with the form.

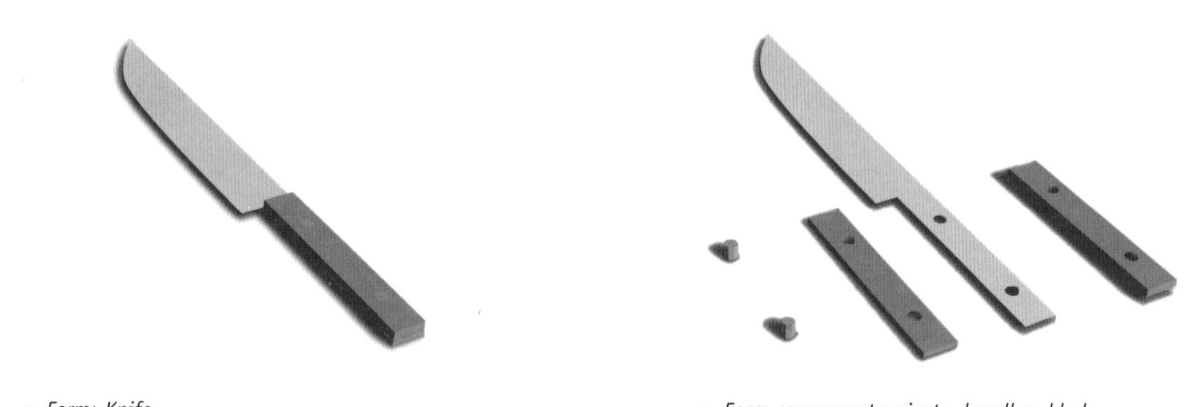

> Form: Knife

> Form components: rivets, handles, blade

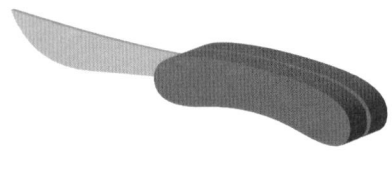

> Knife

> Knife

> Knife

Independently of the individual variants, we abstract the form ("knife"). This is usually enough. It is only when we have a deeper interest in knives, for example because we want to evaluate them, that the form components start to matter. Is the blade too short in relation to the handle? Are the rivets too big? Would it not be better to use mother-of-pearl rather than wood for the handle? This evaluation process is always played out against the background of the recognized "knife" form; the knife does not become a wooden spoon or a chair.

> *Induction*

If there are a few branches sticking up above a wall we can already "see" a tree. Of course we don't see a complete tree, we can't make out where the branches start, or its bark, and yet we are not in any doubt that there is a tree on the other side of the wall. Perceiving important form components (e.g. branches) within a specific set of surroundings [5] permits direct conclusions about a certain form; we immediately "see" a tree. This ability to think of the whole thing immediately even though only parts of it are visible is called induction. [6]. We constantly draw inductive conclusions in everyday life when – on the basis of our prior experience – we complete something in our mind that is only incompletely "portrayed" on our retina. Induction is a resource of our right hemisphere; we take it completely for granted, but it guarantees that we can quickly get our bearings in a fragmentary world.

[5] *Shapes/form components that crop up in an unusual context lead to disturbances (cf. movements in fine art).*

[6] *Current research in neurology (brain research) reinforce the assumption that "seeing" and "thinking" are the same.*

    tr e

Form components are part of a form with a higher grade of superization (e.g. swing in a playground): they give us clues for identifying form rapidly. At the same time, form components are forms in their own right, assimilating the results of a previous superization step (e.g. the swing consisting of supports, ropes, seat etc.).

▬ Forming, design

Forming, or design, creates form, formulates links. Forming as design is implicitly based on the rule that each forming or design component must be examined to establish whether it is suitable for further superization steps. The context is the intellectual background that forming is played out against. Ideally, this applies right down to the bench in the very back corner and its screws. At the same time the object to be designed, a garden, for example, is willy-nilly itself a form component within a larger context (quarter, town, environment etc.) and should relate to that.

The "superization ladder" from the smallest unit to forms of ever-greater complexity, i.e. steps of diversity linked by order relations, forms the conceptual basis for every design activity.

It is also an essential quality criterion when planning landscape architecture projects.

> Connection and landscape architecture projects

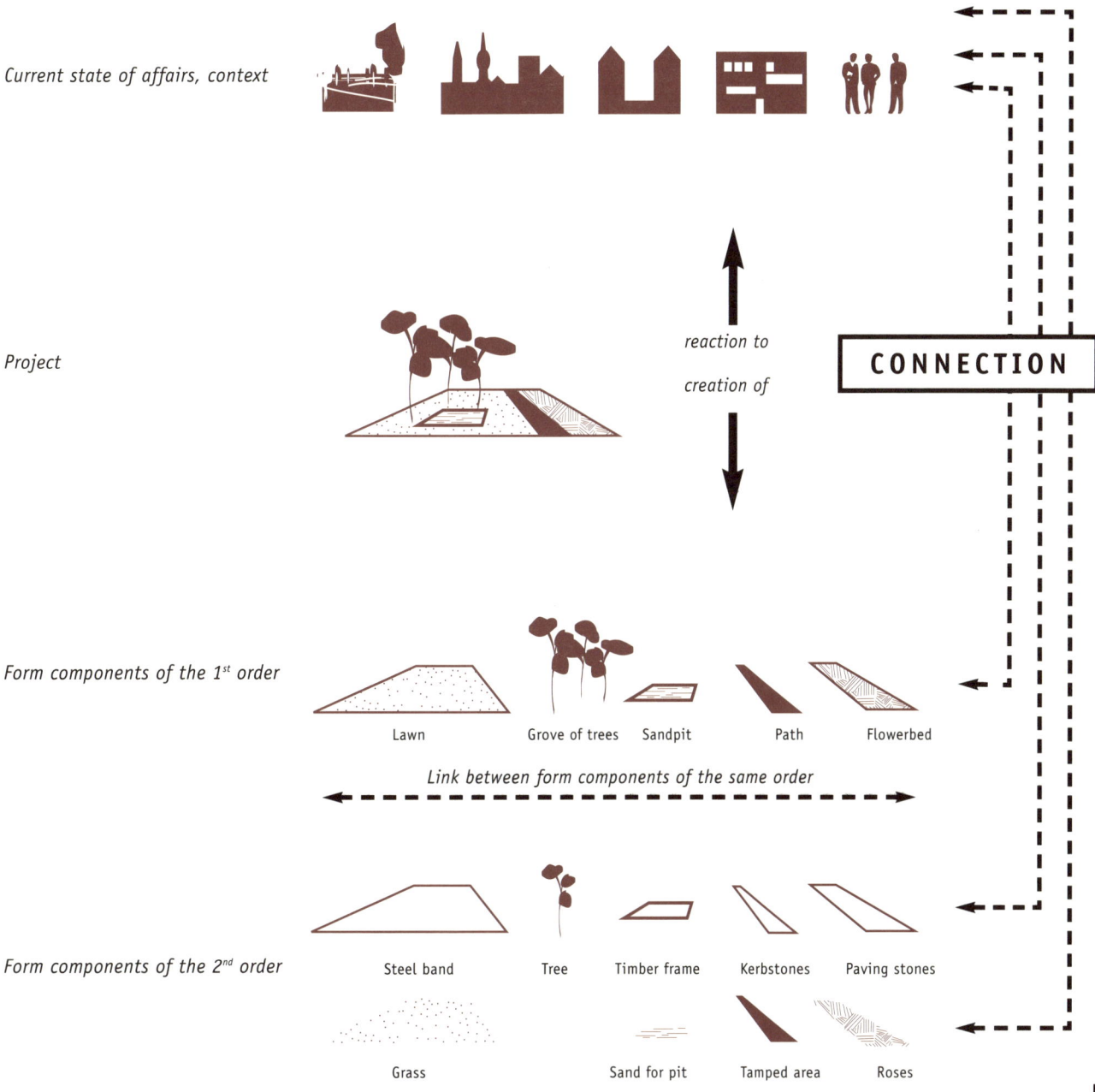

notes

ideas

quotations

sketches

questions

additions

[2] Designing and design

Designing is forming, a creative activity aiming to develop form (connection, coherence). Unlike fine art projects (e.g. sculpture), which are usually manageable and dealt with directly (1:1), the scale of (landscape) architecture projects fundamentally requires the preparatory intermediate step of a symbolic representation (a design in signs) as an abstraction of future reality.

I have always been singled out as someone whom luck has particularly smiled upon; I too do not want to complain, and would not scold about the course my life has taken. However, at bottom it has been nothing but wearisome work, and I can well say that in my 75 years I have had not 4 weeks of actual contentment. It has been the constant shifting of a stone that had ever to be raised again.

J. W. Goethe

Between head and hand

Designing is a dynamic process, by a constant swing from head to hand, from idea to sign, and back again. Every line, every point that we place on a sheet of paper (or create on a computer) is part of our attempt to relate to an idea in our head, every time we create an area we are compelled to examine its potential for becoming part of a certain form (context) that is just developing [7]. Designing is an endless loop of simultaneously evolving drawing development processes and decisions relating to ultimate form.

[7] At the same time every visualized element, every pencil stroke that has slipped contains the possibility of becoming a new starting-point, effectively the basis for a new design (form) idea.

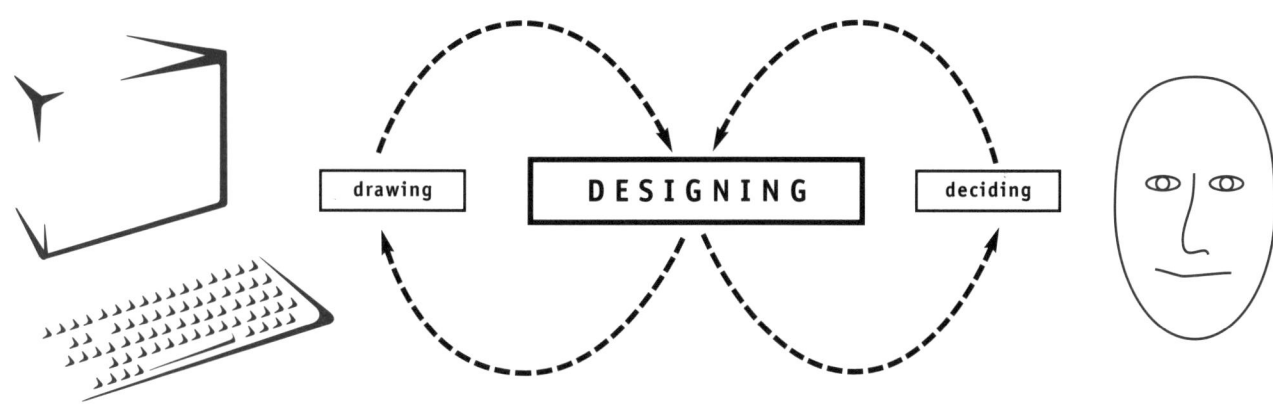

Designing

Designing is not a "god-given" ability, we are not kissed by the Muses (any longer) [8]. On the contrary: designing is a never-ending apprenticeship, is observing, trying, and thinking things over. Designing is a (creative) craft: even in the field of design there are certain decision-making criteria based on a generally recognized body of knowledge or experience (objective criteria for finding form) [9]. In the design process these "objective" criteria become instructions that show the designer how to proceed, they determine that certain

[8] According to Greek mythology, the Muses, daughters of Zeus, were the bringers of creativity, the "divine", of inspiration.
[9] In cabinet-making for example, rules for timber preparation (drying, gluing, direction of cut etc.). For design: criteria for creating space, determining key points, proportion etc. (cf. here all following sections of this book).

design decisions shall become more probable than others. And yet designing as it is based on a large number of situation-dependent factors [10] is not a process that can be (completely) objectified: the designer's individual prior experience and preferences, and also the cultural and specialist background, the mood of the day or a trade magazine opened "at random", the choice of drawing medium or, where applicable, of partners in the design team: all these factors affect the design process, influence the result. And so design, despite "objective" form-finding criteria to show the way, is a process whose development and outcome, in other words whose precise derivation, can be made comprehensible only to a certain extent.

[10] ... of which there are always too few available, and usually the more insignificant ones ....

'A sculptor is working on a large block of granite. He hacks away at the formless block every day. One day a little boy comes by and says, 'What are you looking for?' 'Wait and see,' answers the sculptor. After a few days the little boy comes back, and now the sculptor has carved a beautiful horse out of the granite. The boy stares at it in amazement, then he turns to the sculptor and says, 'How did you know it was in there?''

in: Jostein Gaarder, Sophie's World

▬ The Design

The end of the design process is the design outcome (the design). The design is future form communicated on a symbolic level; designers use it to convey the design idea. So third parties must be able to understand designs (intersubjectivity); this applies both to assessment by clients or specialist juries, and also to the realization phase: as landscape architects do not construct their own work, the design and its further detailing is ultimately a set of building instructions.

> *Intersubjectivity*

Designing (the activity) and design (the result) require that communicable and comprehensible forming criteria be known and applied; these make designs comprehensible, and thus open to meaningful discussion.

The concept of intersubjectivity comes from scientific theory. In fact designing as an activity is similar to scientific working methods in some ways: like these, designing is (also) an empirical process, in other words an activity that aims to acquire insights through observation and experiment; both science and design need intersubjectivity to convey their insights.

The difference between an insight acquired by scientific work and a design lies in how the path that leads to the result is comprehended: scientific statements are characterized by the fact that (theoretically) all the circumstances bringing about the result are (have to be) precisely defined and stated. They are thus (in principle) open to examination by third parties and can be reconstructed exactly, i.e. anyone who follows the steps described "has to" achieve the same result. This is not possible in the case of a design: the design process always has far fewer "objective" form-creating criteria, too many variables that are scarcely communicable and cannot be represented ("subjective" form-creating criteria) for it to be possible for them to be reconstructed "just like that, and not in any other way". And so communicating, conveying designs has to be restricted to mere comprehensibility.

Intention

As human beings, we always move within contexts; we look for them and need them. This applies to superizing individual signs in order to create form and also to more abstract phenomena of our existence: we constantly move within social, family, public etc. contexts and judgements. "Being-in-the-world, as no-longer-being-in-the-mother" [11] compels us to look for other reference systems, make new connections, it requires us – whether we like it or not – to become part of our various contexts.

[11] Cf. Sloterdijk, P.: "Kosmische Quartiere" in: Lettre 46/II 9.

Intention is the meaning, the sense, the view that lies behind our design decisions: what value does it have in a context (formal, historical, philosophical, artistic, social etc.) – that is important to the designer? What is it intended to achieve, what is to be expressed? Landscape architecture is a creative activity that intends to bring about (local) changes to reality. It thus "automatically" adopts a perceptible position, a (formative) standpoint within a specific context: it is (of course) a contribution made within a cultural discourse. Creating form [12] is the plane of mediation between the designer's intention and the recipient's (user's, critic's) interpretation; seen in this way, it is a subtle form of communication that refers to contexts metaphorically, [13] symbolically.

[12] Actually: offering physical interventions, situative opportunities so that the users can create form for themselves. For simplicity's sake we will continue to use the concept of "creating form (Gestaltbildung)" for the landscape architect's activity (cf. also p. 46:"Creating space").

[13] Metaphorical in the sense of not actual, transferred in contrast with direct, actual definition of an object or theme. Something similar applies to almost any form of artistic expression (poetry, painting, music, film etc.).

Creativity

Design operates in the area between designers' decisions based on intersubjective insights and their subjective (individual) intentions and intuitions [14], between "objective" and "subjective" form-creating criteria. Design is always necessary when we (can) know far too little to be able to move compellingly (i.e. on the basis of "if-

[14] Intuition: the ability to identify phenomena in a specific context as essential, without being able to make the reason for this evident.

then" conclusions) from requirements to solutions, in other words when functional intelligence [15] is no longer enough. Creative intelligence is almost complementary to functional intelligence. For creative thinking a (temporary) enhancement of complexity it typical (and necessary): more and more information is added, more and more possible links between the individual pieces of information are being examined and developed. Creativity means the search for potential connections that have not yet been discovered, arising from re-organizing, re-bundling information. The design process is determined by functional and creative intelligence, by compelling and complex, left- and right-hemisphere thinking; it oscillates between multiplication (enhancing complexity) and reduction (reducing complexity, search for links).

[15] *Functional intelligence: the ability to be able to separate components from an unmanageable complex of pieces of information until those remaining are open to legitimate definition. The reduction of diversity leads to insight.*

> Bifurcation

Design is the search for connection using complexological ("chaotic") means: on the way to form, variety is increased to the point where a new superization step "has to" be taken, where parts of the jumble "suddenly" condense to form a new coherence (a form, or gestalt).

Non-linear dynamics is a relatively new science that examines how systems behave relative to the parameters (forces) that affect them. Bifurcations (forkings) [16] are phenomena that occur when systems suddenly change from one state to another as a result of changes in the parameters that constitute them. States before and after bifurcation cannot be unambiguously derived from each other. In the design process, bifurcation means the point of "redemption", of "aha!", it is the recognition of coherence and form [17].

[16] *Cf. www.nld.physik.uni-mainz.de*
[17] *All this applies only to "high-energy systems far from equilibrium" (Ilya Prigogone). And we are nothing else.*

> *The usual design path*

> Design problem, prevailing conditions, concept, aims

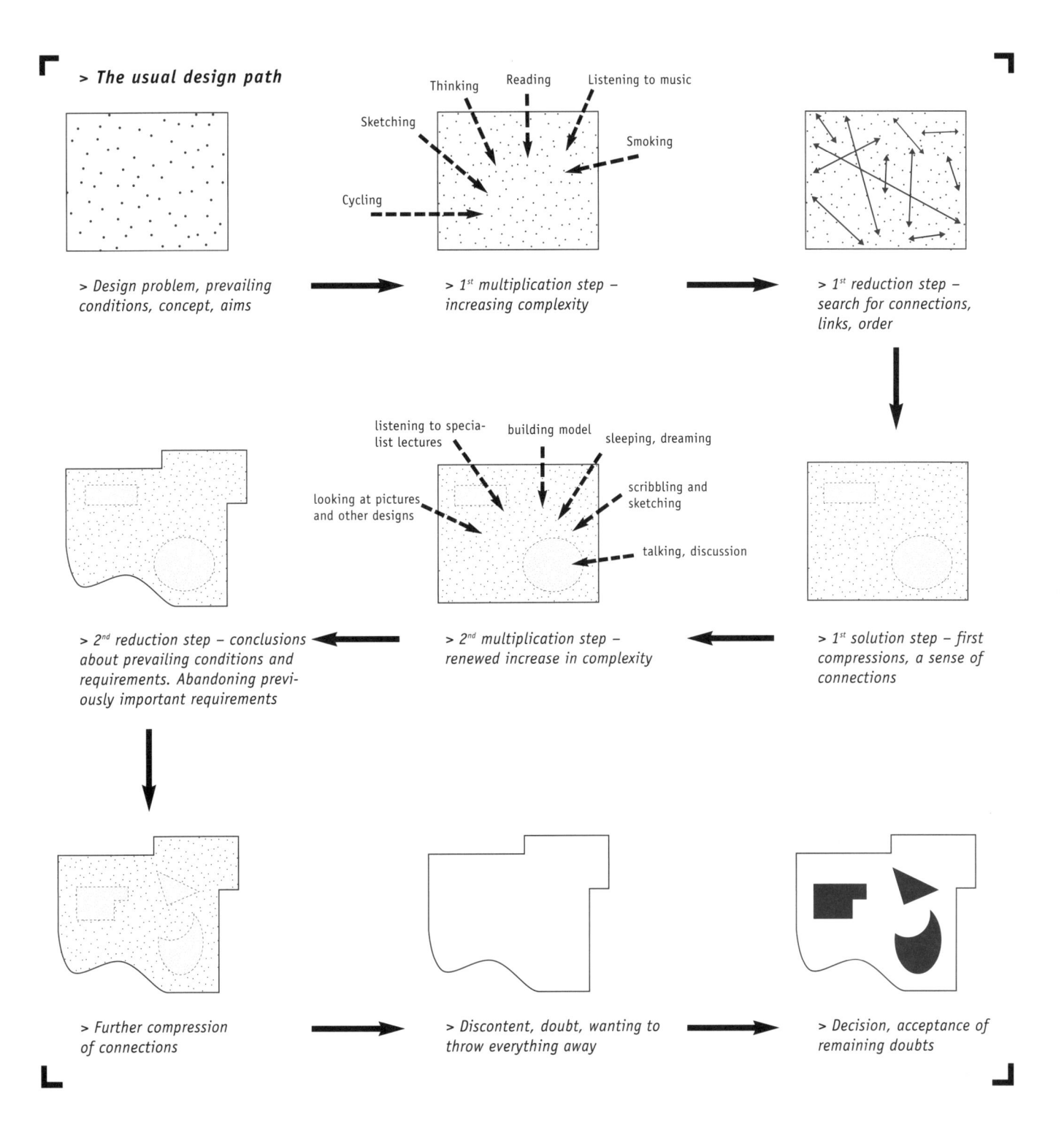

1st multiplication step – increasing complexity
- Thinking
- Reading
- Listening to music
- Sketching
- Smoking
- Cycling

> 1st multiplication step – increasing complexity

> 1st reduction step – search for connections, links, order

> 2nd reduction step – conclusions about prevailing conditions and requirements. Abandoning previously important requirements

> 2nd multiplication step – renewed increase in complexity
- listening to specialist lectures
- building model
- sleeping, dreaming
- looking at pictures and other designs
- scribbling and sketching
- talking, discussion

> 1st solution step – first compressions, a sense of connections

> Further compression of connections

> Discontent, doubt, wanting to throw everything away

> Decision, acceptance of remaining doubts

35

> Working model for the design process (Darke, Lawson)

A mid-seventies field experiment observed a number of established designers during a design process. It emerged that there is a very close "probably inseparable connection between the analysis and the synthesis stage" [18] in the design process: individual aspects of the problem (requirements) and concrete possible solutions emerging as a direct reaction to these make up the actual individual working steps, the "molecules" of the design process for experienced designers.

[18] Cf. Darke, J., "The primary generator and the design process" in: Rogers/Ittelsson (ed.): "New directions in environmental design research", Washington, EDRA 1978.

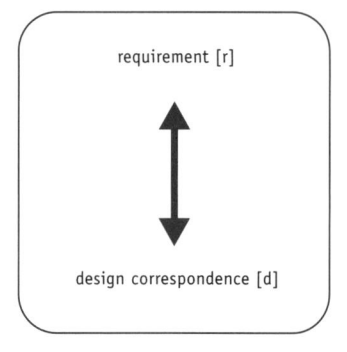

> Individual aspect of a solution

> Solution (form) as a whole

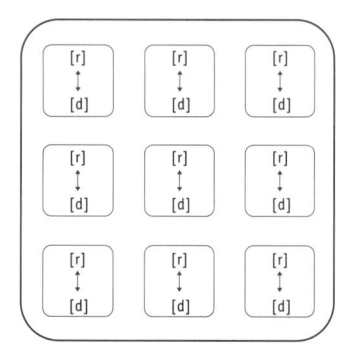

Working on the basis of Darke's study, B. Lawson [19] developed a working model for architectural design processes. Here he distinguishes between three requirement dimensions: situational requirements (internal situational requirement: interplay between parts of the object to be designed; external situational requirement; interplay with the context); person responsible for requirements (designer himself, client, user, legislator); meaning (sense, reason) of or for the requirements (radical: value placed by the designer or the users; practical: structural-constructive standards, maintenance, use; formal: shape, form-rules and -qualities; symbolic: model, idea, mood, theme etc.).

[19] Cf. Lawson, B., "Science, legislation and architecture" in: Evans/Powel/Talbot (ed.): "Changing design", New York, J. Wiley, 1980.

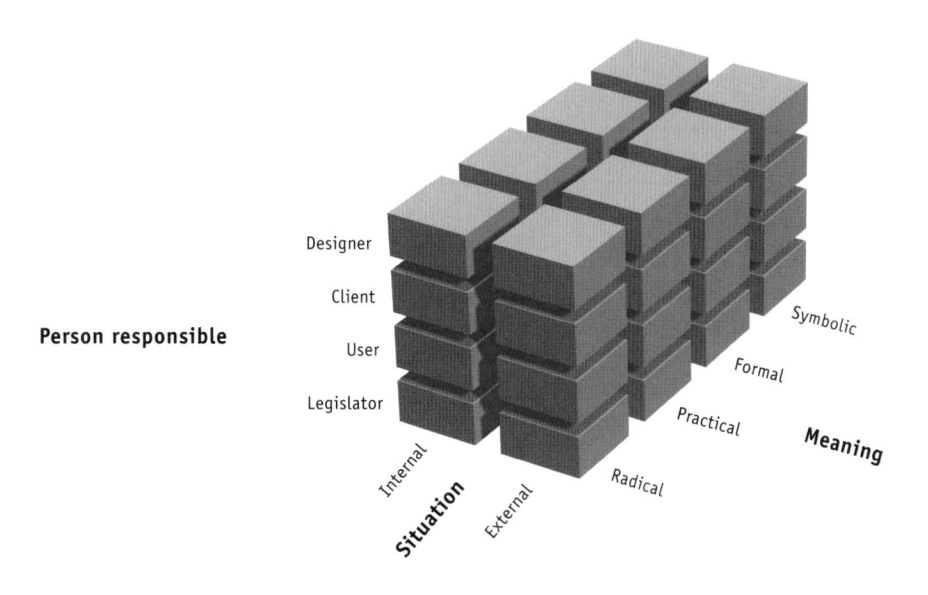

> Working model for design processes (according to Lawson)

Means and end

Designing landscape architecture means thinking about future form in advance, devising it and making it more precise. Given the almost constitutive uncertainty of the design process it is highly improbable that there will be one solution to a problem. It is more likely that various design routes and intentions will offer design solutions that are perhaps formally different, but similarly convincing in relation to a stated requirement).

For this reason a design is never "right", but it is more or less good with regard to the specific demands made on it. "Right" would mean: building up a design from unambiguous, compelling connections that exclude all other solutions ("if-then" conclusions) [20], whereas "good" expresses the intersubjective comprehensibility and credibility of the form-creating decisions. A good design is a convincing one. Seldom there is but one, the "best" design, but one, the best way: there are usually several good solutions that can satisfactorily meet a specific bundle of requirements (aims).

[20] "Right" is only: two pounds of apples weigh more than one pound of pears.

A professor of physics, a building engineer and a painter are standing by a church tower and trying to estimate its height. A local businessman who is passing suggests a competition: he has just taken delivery of some new, expensive barometers, and to advertise these he offers a prize to the person who establishes the height of the tower most accurately with one of his barometers. All three agree: the professor of physics measures the barometric pressure as accurately as possible using averaged multiple readings, then goes to the top of the tower and makes equally precise measurements; he calculates the height of the tower from the difference. The building engineer scoffs at all this elaborate effort; he goes up the tower, drops the barometer and measures the time it takes to reach the ground with his stopwatch, then quickly calculates the height. To both their surprise, it is the painter who manages to state the height most accurately. He simply goes into the adjacent vicarage and offers the verger the barometer as a present if he will get the building plans for the church out of the library for him; the verger is happy to do that and our painter simply takes the correct quotation for the height of the tower from it.

in E. De Bono, "Teach thinking"

▬ Prevailing conditions

The creative freedom of work on landscape architecture is usually constrained at a very early stage by defined aims and prevailing conditions: this includes definite wishes expressed by the people initiating the planning and the future users and also the particular qualities of the context (e.g. ground water level, local climate, character of the surrounding buildings, building use etc.) and legal requirements (e.g. nature conservation, protection of historic monuments, fire regulations etc.). Thinking about and if necessary re-evaluating such requirements is the first and often the crucial step in the design process: it is only by creatively revealing the actual demands behind supposedly indispensable design requirements (prevailing conditions) that makes it possible to establish what the actual design problems are.

Design means making possibilities into necessities. An intellectual fishing-net, knotted together from the planning initiators' demands, from use advantages and from the stories the location can tell, hauls the first set of material out of a sea of possibilities: ideas, form (arche-)types and models. Some fit together well, form the first structure, need each other. Taking these up, completing them, extending, reducing, linking, refining and sharpening detail until an overall form of maximum intellectual and formal consistency emerges, until all the parts and the whole become even more intensely coherent, even more concrete, that is what making possibilities into necessities means. From freedom to subservience, that is design (and life).

A good design stands out because it makes us understand the "necessity" of a certain form for a specific place (intersubjectively),

i.e. it can communicate this necessity convincingly.

As though (almost) no other solution would be possible in this location.

▬ Sign and Content

Designing is the path to inventing form, the design is form shorthand for future reality. Designing anticipates three-dimensional solutions, using the limited representational resources of the second dimension [21]. The ultimate aim of the work is not the image (the design) but the altered local reality. Thus designing requires the ability to "see" two-dimensional points, lines and areas as solids, in other words to understand their three-dimensional effect immediately.

[21] Models as abstracted miniaturizations are also a possible way of finding form. But in landscape architecture they are usually only used as first means for spatial analysis or as complementary control devices, as it is very difficult to convey the complexity of human scale in miniature form.

Every line that we draw in a design stands for a three-dimensional, spatial/solid reality.

> ***This horizontal projection . . .***

. . . can mean all this (and presumably more as well):

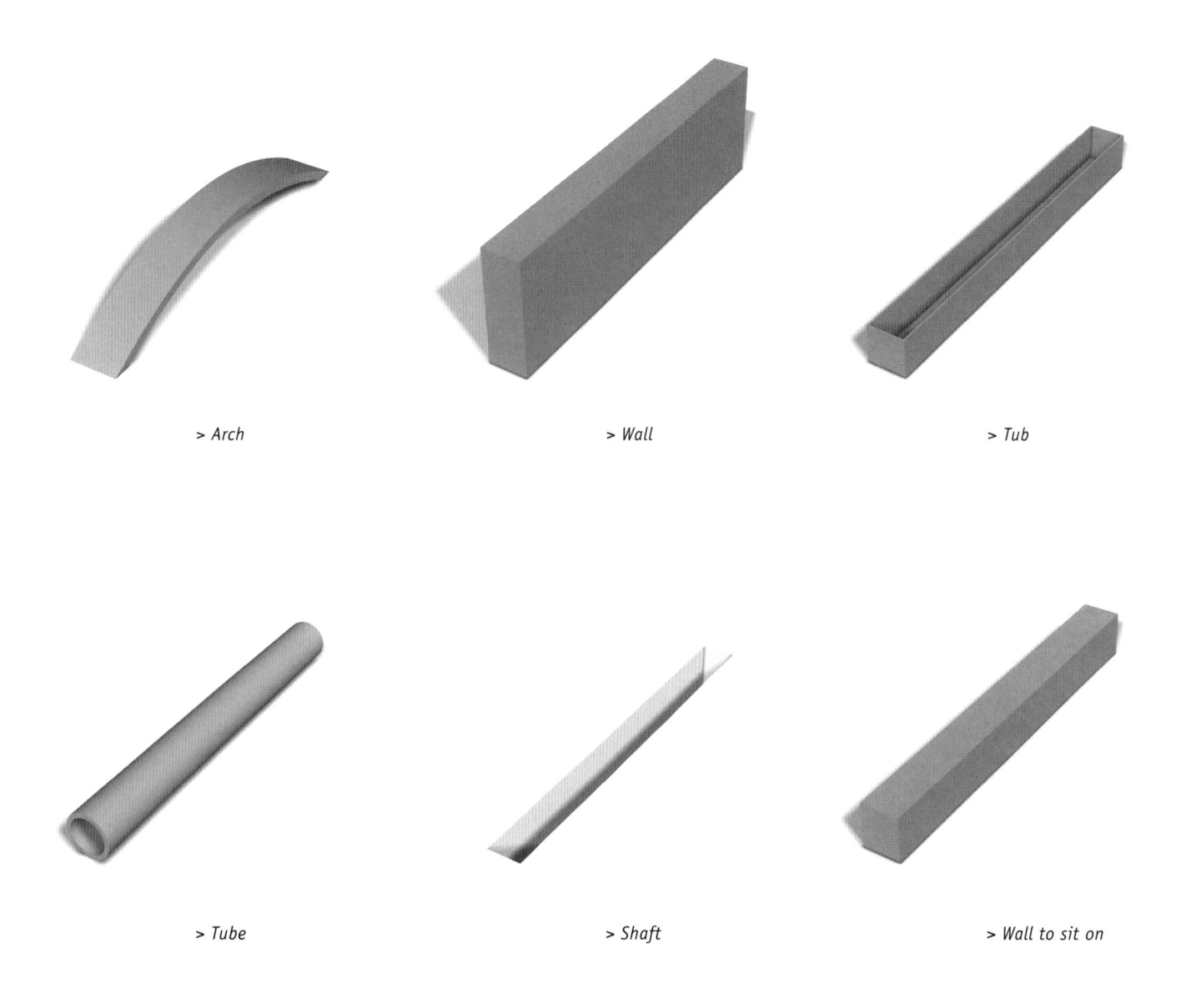

> Arch

> Wall

> Tub

> Tube

> Shaft

> Wall to sit on

notes

ideas

quotations

sketches

questions

additions

[3] Space - place - path

3.1 Creating space ("space")

3.2 Selecting the focal point ("place")

3.3 Movement and access ("path")

3.1 Creating space ("space")

For us human beings, creating space is a natural, pre-conscious act of self-positioning within our surroundings.

Landscape architecture, which deals with changing such surroundings, defines itself by responding to this phenomenon: what the landscape architect does is to relate things to each other in such a way that they can become spatially effective, and starting-points for mental superization processes (form-space).

Landscape architecture anticipates space creation.

There is not man, and then also space.

O. F. Bollnow

▄ Space

Space is form. The criteria that apply to the generation of form by people (seeking and recognizing coherence with the aid of prior experience) also apply to the phenomenon of space. Creating space is perfectly natural to us human beings, it is an essential act of self-location [22]. The effect and perception of space – unlike the more generally applicable term form – relate to the interior: space is territory, separates "me" from "you", "us" from "the others". The perception of space, interpreting it as "inside", as inclusion, needs (and creates) an "outside", an exclusion. And between these comes the crucial element: the boundary.

[22] Human evolution is based to a large extent on rapid space-distance perception (What do I see? Danger! Where? How far away? What possible response?)

▄ Spaces in landscape architecture

Unlike architectural spaces, landscape-architecture spaces are not covered over, they have no roof [23]. Landscape-architecture projects, i.e. gardens, parks, courtyards, streets etc. all share – independently of their dimensions or appearance – the presence of the sky as a constant companion.

[23] Exception: dense grove of trees. For this cf. p. 85: "the grove"

Landscape architecture creates space between an area, a vertical boundary and the sweep of the sky.

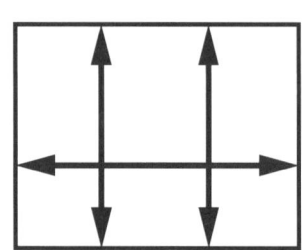

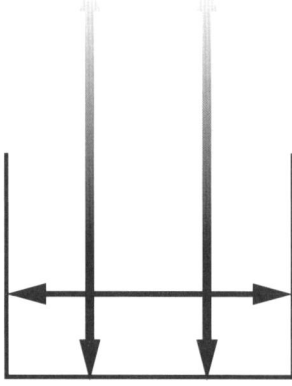

> Architectural space

> Landscape architecture space

▬ 4 propositions for creating landscape architecture space

> *1st proposition: space is area unit and three-dimensional boundary*

> *Area-unit*   + > *Boundary*   = > *Space*

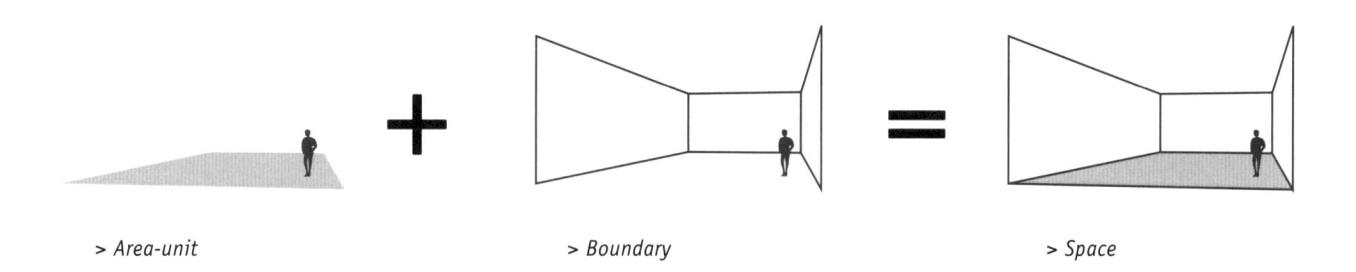

Area-unit and spatial boundary relate to each other reciprocally: the weaker the "spatial boundary" is, the more indistinctly it will function as a space-creating criterion, and the area-unit will have to assert itself all the more "strongly" and clearly (and vice versa). The criteria "weaker" and "stronger" or "clearer" always relate to the degree of unity of area-unit and boundary, or the degree to which they differ from their surroundings.

> *2nd proposition: the weaker the boundary, the stronger the area (and vice versa)*

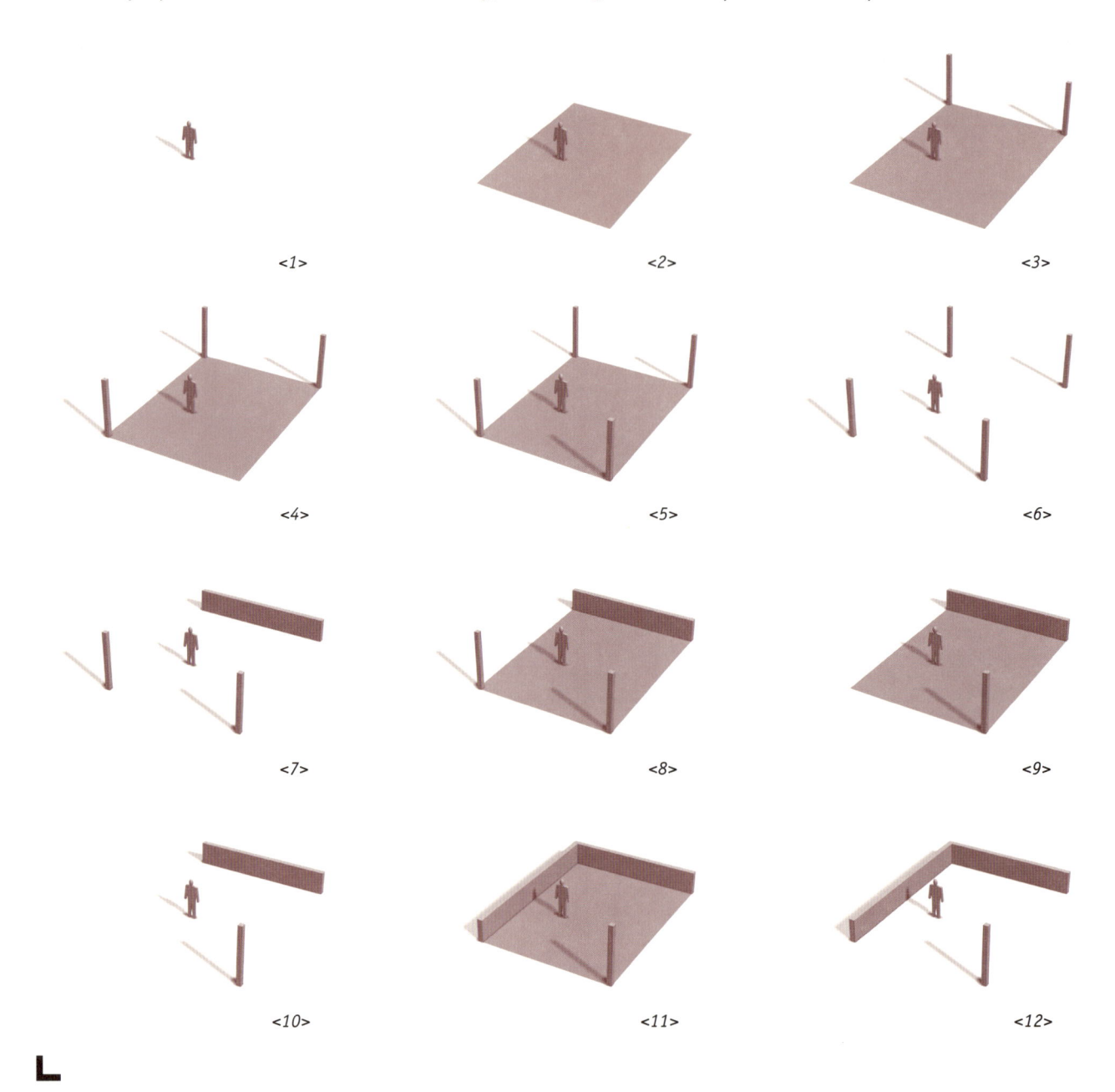

<1>

<2>

<3>

<4>

<5>

<6>

<7>

<8>

<9>

<10>

<11>

<12>

<13> <14> <15>

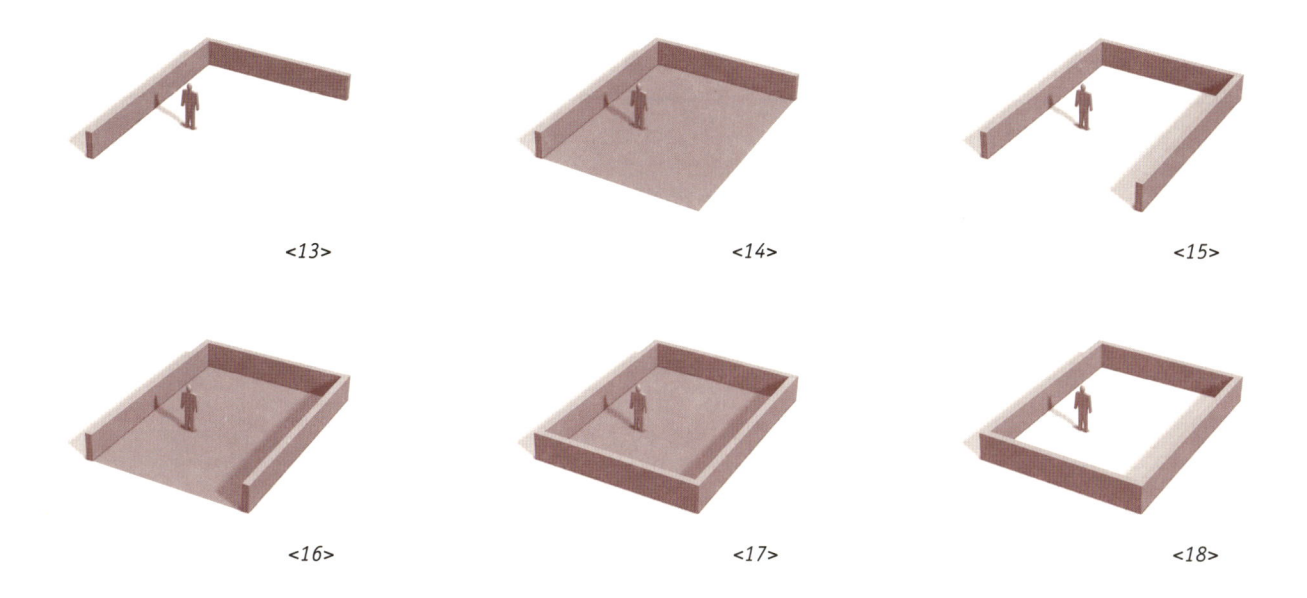

<16> <17> <18>

People need area-units and solid boundary signs in order to be able to create spaces <1>. A unified area-unit cannot create space on its own <2>, it only defines a field (specific area). Solid items placed on the boundaries of an area-unit become increasingly effective spatially <3-5>. In these terms, <3> is still very indistinct, only <4> starts to create an indication of space, and only <5> a distinct space. This immediately becomes indistinct again when the area-unit disappears <6>. Reinforcing a boundary by a continuous boundary wall <7> helps only to a certain extent. When the area-unit is reintroduced, the spatial impression is suddenly very distinct again <8>, it remains effective even when one of the columns is removed <9>, but not without the area-unit <10>. Reinforcing the area-unit with additional, continuous walls on its boundaries strengthens the spatial impression very greatly <11>, so that it remains effective even without its area-unit character <12> (though "weaker"). Removing the last boundary solid creates an indication of space (niche) <13> that is greatly strengthened by area-unity <14> Closing a third side with a wall produces a very clear spatial situation even without an area-unit <15>; the independent area-unit strengthens this even more <16>. Complete closure with boundary walls produces the most independent but also the most insulated space <17>, it no longer needs anything to distinguish its area from the surroundings, as these can no longer be included <18>.

People and space are inseparably linked. The impact of spaces hardly depends on their absolute, measurable size; in fact the nature of the feeling conveyed by the space (cramped/spacious, protected/open etc.) is dependent on both the observer's spatial distance from the solids forming the boundary and on the height difference between the observer's eye-level and the height of the solids. A sense of space is a proportion phenomenon, and its comparative value is human scale.

> **3rd proposition: space means experience of proportion (not of scale)**

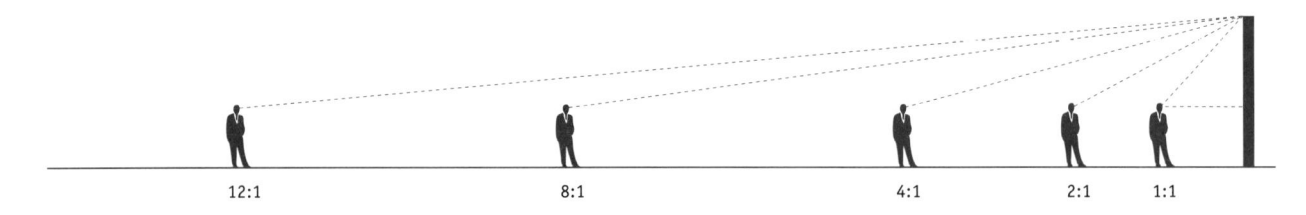

12:1   8:1   4:1   2:1   1:1

> *Spatial effect dependent on the distance between observing subject and observed object*

> *Spatial effect dependent on the relation of the position of the subject's eye and the height of the object*

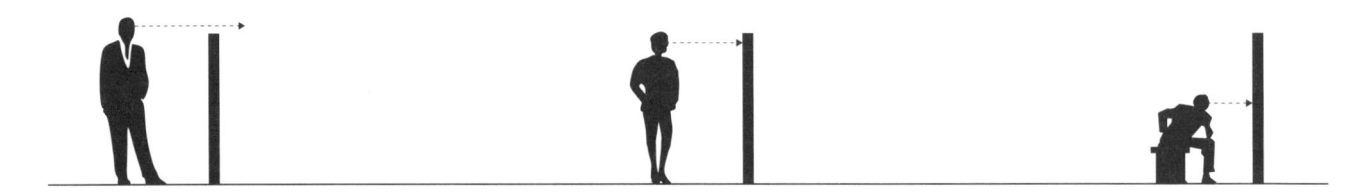

The way we register space, meaning our sense of the size and distance of objects, depends on our prior (visual) experiences, in other words on a habitual relationship between the distance of a body and the size of the "image" of this body on our retina. ▬ The smaller an object whose real size we are aware of seems, the further away it is from us. ▬ Parallel lines running along our line of vision get closer and closer together the further they are away. ▬ Parallel lines running across our line of vision get closer together towards the back (only at a regular distance, otherwise optical illusion). Textures and structures become denser with increasing distance (texture gradient).

> 4th proposition: registering space is prior experience

> *Structures and prior (visual) experience*

> *Disturbing prior experience*

Man opens out his space from the centre in which he stands, always within a bordering, unity-bestowing horizon; the fact that man never reaches his horizon, but that this moves along with him, shows only that the horizon is inseparably attached to man and man always remains the centre of his horizon-enclosed space.

O. F. Bollnow

— "Pure" space

Space is – above all – an orientation category: it is our constant companion "as we wander through the world", helping us to determine and secure our location. Space does not exist without people, because we create it ourselves, "work it out" again (at every moment of our being). For although the world around us changes almost with every step we take [24] we are always looking for (and finding) "space", space to move through, space that surrounds us.

[24] One only has to think of going to work: how many different spaces do we create then?

Space is thus the highest level of abstraction: it is the result of a mental process (presumably involving the right hemisphere) that gets to essentials by reducing diversity: where am I? Here!

"Pure" space is an attempt to depict the (intellectual) construct of human space creation pictorially: space as a self-sufficient, inward-looking structure, characterized by equal, continuously closed boundary walls and a uniform, level surface. Space as a unit. And we are in the middle of it.

> "Pure" space

▬ Breaking down "pure" space

Landscape architecture alters (spatial) realities; it offers local morphological qualities as starting-points for mental superization processes (from multiplicity to unity, from tree to space). Given that sufficient starting points are needed to be able to create space, landscape architecture means work on the boundaries, the areas and the solids within a spatial situation that is to be developed:
▬ Dissolving or reshaping the closed boundary wall of "pure" space are ways of trying to discover and offer a wide range of connections between "inside" (space) and "outside" (context), ▬ modelling, as a morphological disturbance of the uniform, even area creates distinctions and offers situative behavioural opportunities.

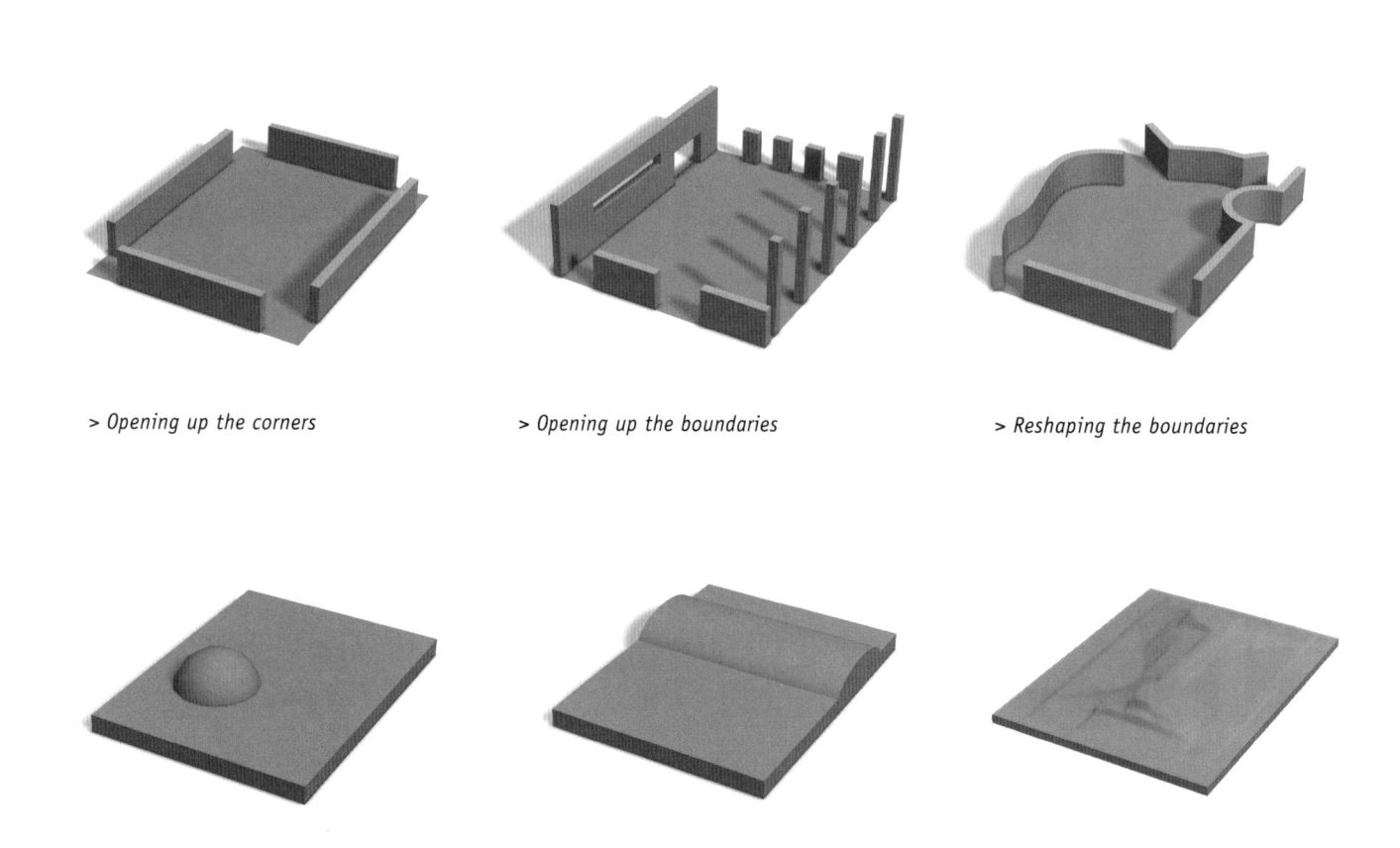

> *Opening up the corners*

> *Opening up the boundaries*

> *Reshaping the boundaries*

> *Point modelling*

> *Linear modelling*

> *Soft modelling*

The more strongly "pure" space is broken down, the more links with the context are offered, the more three-dimensional the area becomes, the more weakly the space becomes perceptible as a coherent, independent unit. The deconstruction of "pure" space reaches its bifurcation point [25] where the boundary between inside and outside, between "me" and "them" breaks down, where solid boundary and area unit cease to create space in a particular location and "suddenly" become components of a different context (that was perhaps not intended by the design).

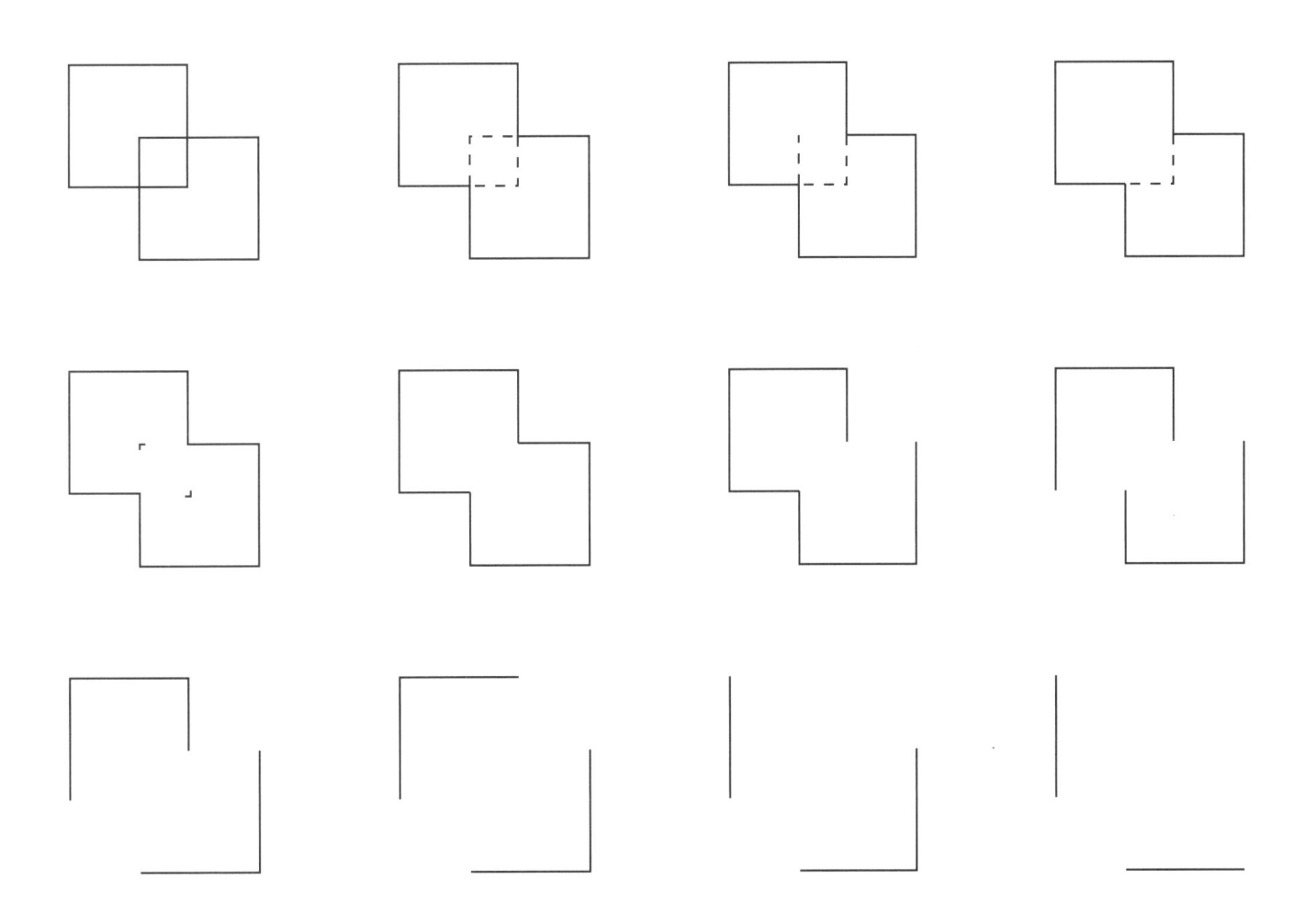

[25] *Bifurcation as the point at which phenomena "suddenly" change from one state into another. Cf. p. 34: "Bifurcation".*

> *Three spaces are worked on successively at their boundaries. From what point can we only make out two spaces, when only one? When is spatial independence completely lost, when do the boundary walls become part of other contexts?*

▬ Suggesting space

Creating space means mentally completing components that can be perceived incompletely [26]. Essential prerequisites for creating

[26] Cf. chap. "Form and forming", p. 21 "Induction".

space are the location (the relation) of the boundary solids to each other, their potential to be summed up theoretically as "space". The more familiar the form of the area unit is in plan (e.g. simple regular shapes like square, circle), the "weaker" the marking of the boundaries or the corners can be; unusual, e.g. irregular or composed ground plan forms need clear, "strong" boundary markings.

> Defining space by (solid) marking of corners or boundary walls

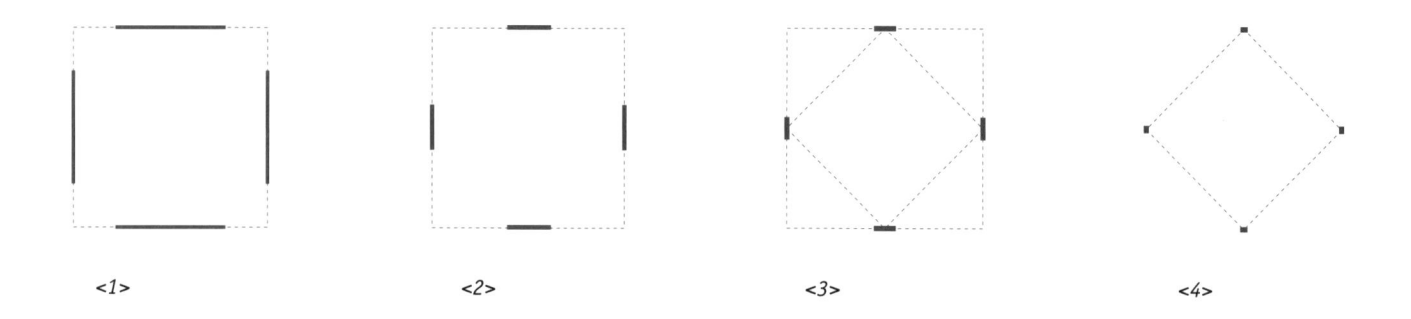

<1>   <2>   <3>   <4>

> "Creating" space by marking the boundary walls – The shorter the boundary walls become, the "weaker" the originally desired spatial situation becomes, and the relationship to the outside becomes "stronger" (<1> and <2>). From a certain moment <3> the spatial creation "swings" between the horizontal and a turn through 45°, between interpreting the boundaries as a boundary wall or corner point. In <4> the space has "tilted" completely, the boundary walls have become corner points.

Suggested spaces are spatial phenomena that lack a clear, solid boundary at crucial points. Suggested spaces (corners, niches or similar) do not "create" a clear inside and outside. On the contrary: the simultaneity of inside and outside, of intimacy and exposure, of being captive or free are among suggested space's characteristic attractions.

The corner is a sort of half-box, partly walls, floor, ceiling, and partly door. It manifests the dialectic of inside and outside.

Martino Gamper

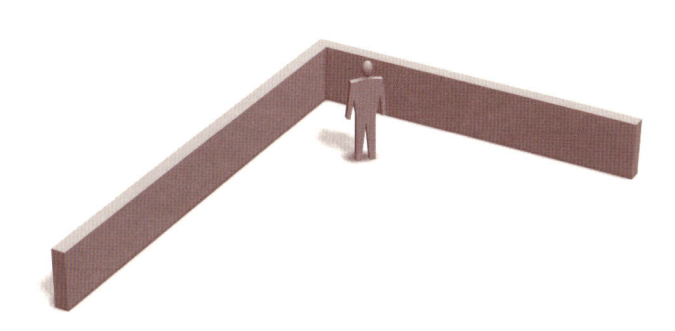

> *Suggested space – increased distance reduces the spatial effect*

Introducing uniform quality to the area or physically marking "missing" space boundaries strengthens the spatial effect; both to-gether go beyond suggestion to create a very clear spatial quality [27].

[27] Cf. also pp. 50-51: "the weaker the boundary, the stronger the area (and vice versa)"

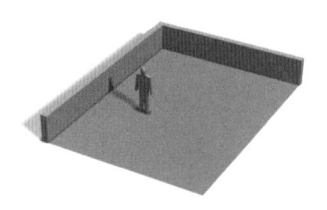

> *Suggested space – "strengthening" by area unity*

> *Space – by marking the "missing" corner*

> *Clear space – marking the "missing" corner and the unity of the area*

> *The corners or niches that are turned away from the viewer are always the ones that are perceived as being "inside", <2> and <3> create relatively clear spatial situations. <1> and <2> are less clear, but more open to the surroundings*

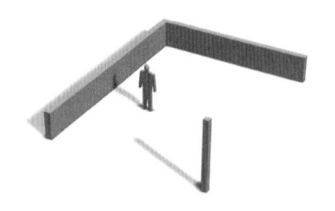

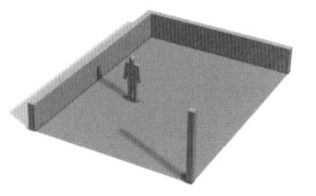

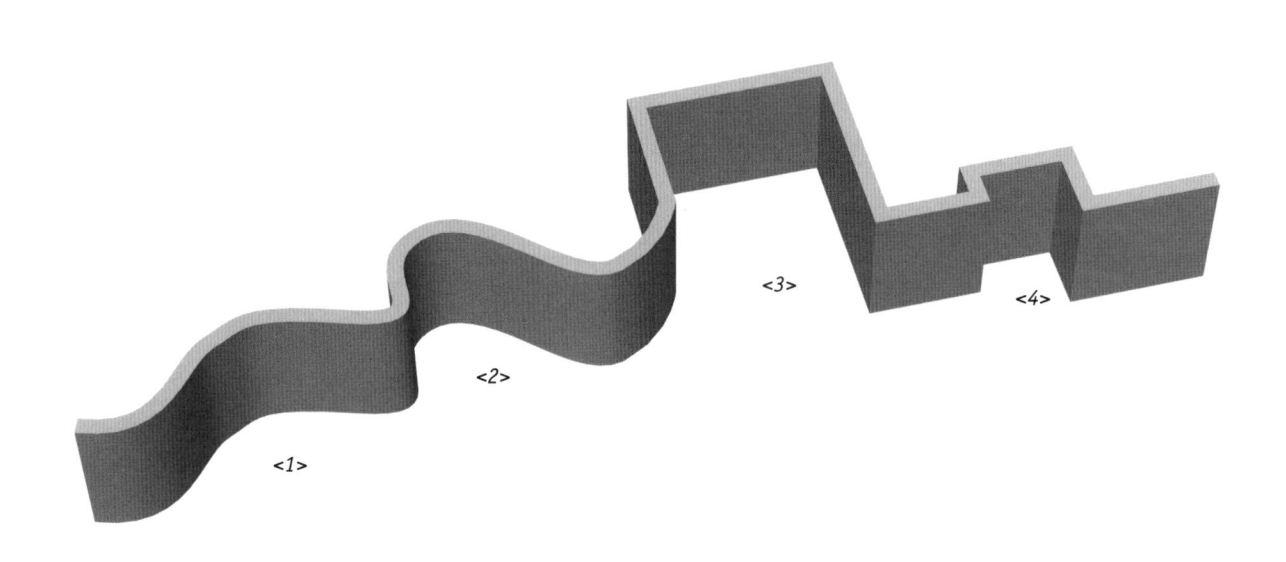

>Two trees – different spaces

Situation: building set back in a tree-lined street, an exit. Aim: to create a square in front of it. Instrument: two trees.

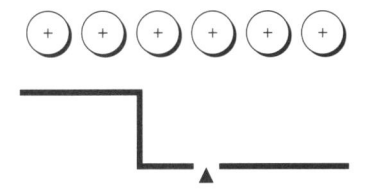

> Existing situation

> Two small spaces in front extending up to the road

> Two spaces in front extending up to the edge of the building

> Tiny (almost private) space in front and larger, public, space

> Division into public and semi-private zone (without emphasizing the entrance)

> Large, inviting, essentially public space without emphasizing the entrance

> Strong, public emphasis on the entrance – inviting

> Space on the street side, closed, private portal at the entrance. Emphasizes the entrance without being inviting

> Coherent space marking the entrance

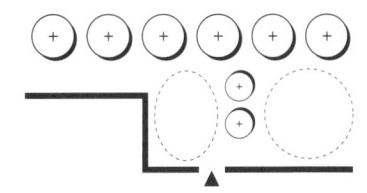

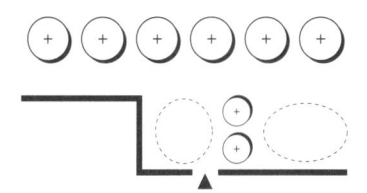

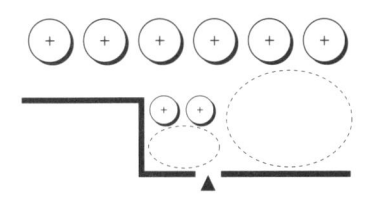

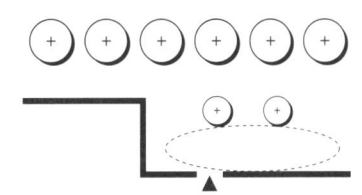

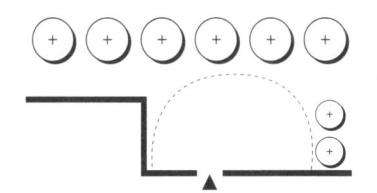

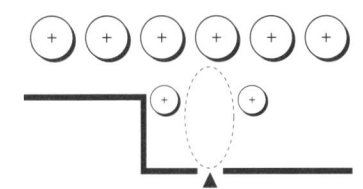

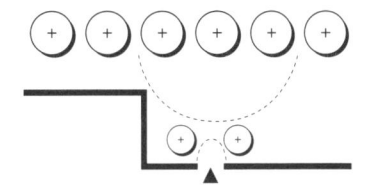

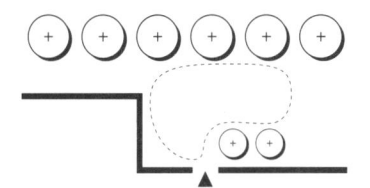

▬ Spatial sequences – spatial gradations

▬ Spatial sequences are connected, independent spatial situations that refer to each other through their access links; only one space can be perceived at any one time. In contrast with this, ▬ spatial gradations are spatial situations encapsulated inside each other. For the viewer several space boundaries (of different kinds/strength) are usually recognizable at the same time. The access has little significance as a means of reading the space.

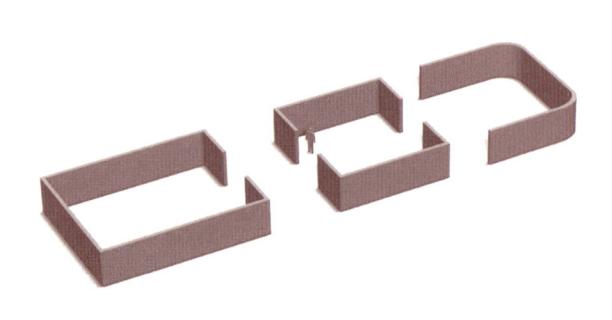

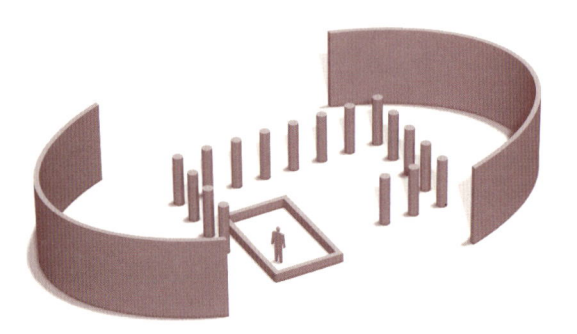

> *Spatial sequences*

> *Spatial gradations*

▬ From closed to open spaces

Landscape architecture tries to discover and promote links between "inside" (space) and "outside" (context). Working on boundaries is the principal instrument that can be used to this end. ▬**Closed spaces** with continuous boundary walls shut themselves off from their surroundings, all the more so the higher and denser they are. They are self-sufficient, and do not seek connections with the outside world. ▬**Boundary openings** create committed, more or less clearly directed connections with the surroundings; they focus movement and sightlines. ▬**Transparent spatial boundaries** make free but random (non-directional) connections with the surroundings. They make spaces seem bigger, but they are very dependent on context for their content. ▬**Open spatial boundaries** are created by isolated items placed along the boundary of the area-unit. Their ability to create space effectively depends on the distances between the individual items and the degree of area uniformity. Open spatial boundaries create free connecting zones, and links with the outside are focused by the size of the "gap" and/or the special nature of the items (e.g. gates).

> Closed/dense spatial boundary (boundary wall)

> Boundary opening

> Transparent boundary

> Open boundaries

▬ Spatial boundaries

Spatial boundaries can be created in a variety of ways. ▬Uniform, solid boundary walls can be achieved by using buildings, walls, fences, hedges, height differences (modelling, terracing) etc. ▬Composite boundaries are created by arranging different elements along a boundary line: single trees, solitaire shrubs, entwined structures, items of furniture (benches, lamps, fire brigade bollards), stones, strips of wall, single mounds etc.

Uniformity of area

The effectiveness of areas for spatial perception is dependent on their unity (similarity) and how distinct they are from their surroundings. The greater the uniformity and the more marked the contrast with their surroundings, the more definitely an area will be seen as coherent. Area uniformity can be achieved by everything: ▬ flat green structures (lawn, fields with long grass, ground cover, flowerbeds etc.) ▬ "hard" surface coverings (brickwork, paving, asphalt, concrete, steel plates etc.) ▬ "soft" surface coverings (compacted gravels, sand, plastic pavers, water etc.).

Differences from the surrounding area can be produced by ▬ different colours ▬ brightness differences (light against dark materials, but also: sunny as opposed to shady spaces during the day, lit as opposed to unlit areas at night; full shade under a chestnut as opposed to half-shade under a robinia etc.) ▬ structural or textural differences (fine-grained sand vs. coarse chippings, lawn vs. sand, rounded sand vs. angular chippings, mosaic pavement vs. large slabs etc.).

> Spatial size dependent on human proximity

Social psychologists are concerned with the phenomenon of "space" in its relationship with human proximity. E.T. Hall identifies four categories of social distance [28]: **_Intimate distance** means less than 0.5 metres between people. Only people we are very close to are accepted within this distance without tension, information conveyed by touch (tactile) and smell (olfactory) is more important than sight.

[28] Hall, E.T., "The hidden dimension".

_Personal distance means 0.5 to 1 metres between people. This corresponds roughly to the instinctive protective circle around a person. People can be discerned by peripheral vision (150° angle of sight) and their movements registered. Olfactory and tactile information plays a part, but optical perception is already dominant. Within personal distance, strangers are kept at a tension-free distance by instinctively moving away; if this is not possible, the result is a breakdown of communication and feelings ranging from uncertainty to fear, strain or defencelessness. Examples: travelling in a lift that is full already or on crowded public transport, strangers in a restaurant at the same (small) table or on a park bench.

Most social contacts with other people occur within **_social distance**. This means a distance of 1 to 2.5 metres (close social distance) and 2.5 to 5 metres (greater social distance). Within social distance a person can be observed through their physical activity; perception is almost totally visual and acoustic. When designing spaces in which strangers are intended to interact, it helps to maintain social distance (especially greater social distance) when arranging individual positions (benches, table widths, playing positions etc.). If the distances are less than this there will be tension, aggression or unease, but also – on the positive side – greater pressure to communicate. Pressure to communicate clearly decreases over greater social distance [29].

[29] Social distance carries a marked urge to communicate, when engaged in uncommunicative activities (e.g. reading) it leads to a feeling of uneasiness, and people instinctively tend to distance themselves from strangers more.

_Public distance covers the area of 5 to 7 (10) metres; the upper limit can differ according to cultural, social or personal factors. To make contact with people we know, either the distance is reduced or special signs (waving, calling out etc.) are used. Maintaining public distance from strangers is a clear sign of resistance to spontaneous communication.

Example: people gradually start to occupy a sunbathing lawn with low boundaries (long grass, shrubs, low wall or similar). It is early afternoon, not very hot, there is a tree at the south-western end.

Where will people choose to be?

Figures 1-15 show the most probable places for them to occupy.

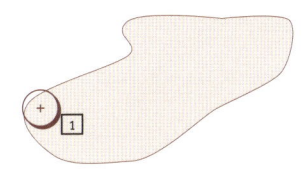

> Most attractive because of the tree (protection, roof, focal point).

> People occupy the boundary areas next. Suggested niches act as "key condensation points".

> To maintain public distance, people occupy the normally unattractive middle (cf. distribution of people in restaurants or cafés).

> All the people who arrive subsequently have to come to terms with greater social distance

> And so on…

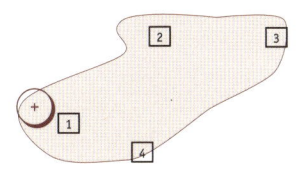

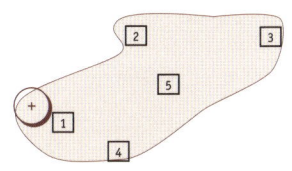

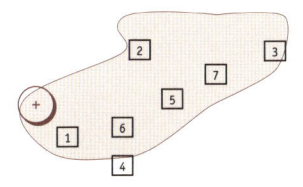

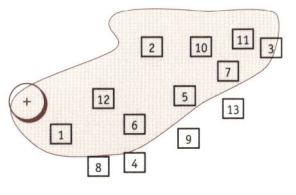

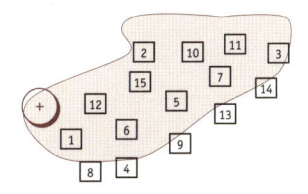

Greater density (involving close social distance) is highly improbable and will normally be avoided. But if it does happen, for example on a hot day on the beach, there will be changes of behaviour and a clearly imposition of boundaries on personal territory (using towels, beach huts, turning one's back etc.).

Space and the effect of space

Spaces support associations, they evoke moods and states of mind. A number of conditions affect the mood that a particular spatial unit evokes in us. But many of these are not, or only to a limited extent, within the landscape architect's sphere of influence: classical "moodmakers" like the weather, the seasons or the time of day are factors here, and so are temporary events (e.g. a low-flying aircraft over a lake, a deer grazing on the edge of a wood etc.) or the viewer's subjective state [30]. The limited scope available to landscape architecture in influencing mood can be set against these conditions that cannot be influenced (yet?); alongside **material qualities**, in other words the nature and characteristics of the materials used, the chief factor here is playing with **proportion**, in other words the ratio between the viewer's distance from a spatial boundary and that between the point of sight and the height of the boundary [31].

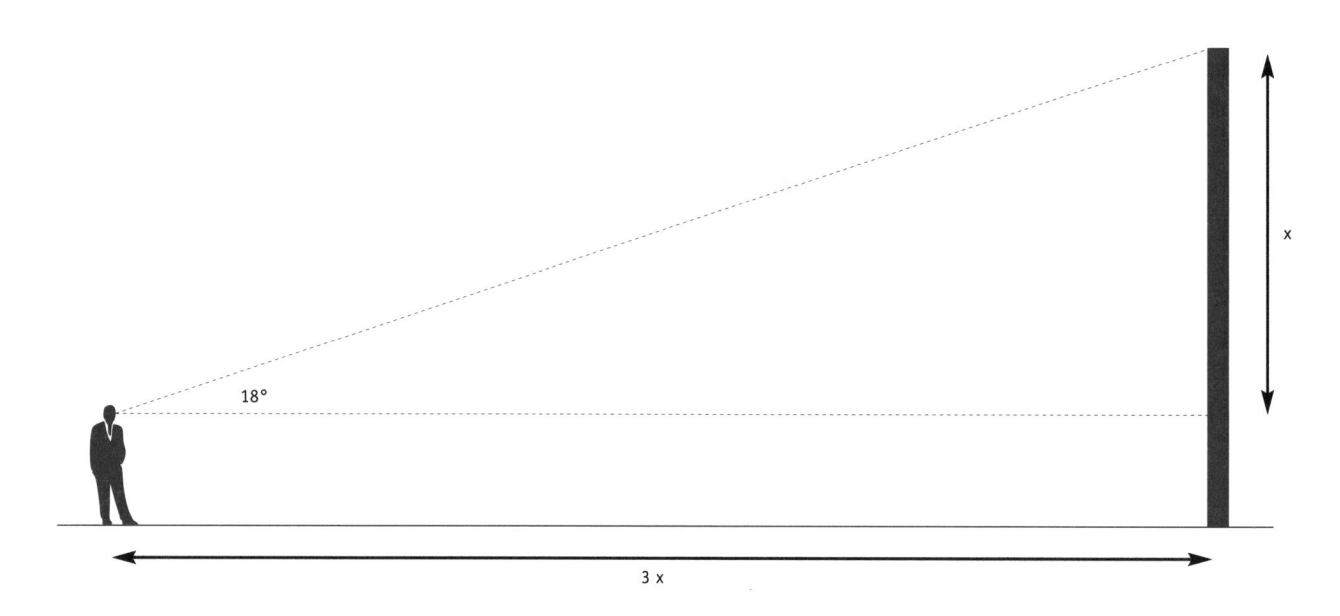

[30] *Just like any other form, any other "sign", spaces do not stand "for themselves", but are interpreted in the context of prior experience.*

[31] *Cf. p. 52: "Space means experience of proportion (not of scale)".*

> *Ratio 3:1 (x = height of the object minus the observer's eye-level)*

This produces another ratio that helps to determine the impact made by the landscape architecture feature: the ratio between the height of the boundary and the piece of sky that can be seen above it.

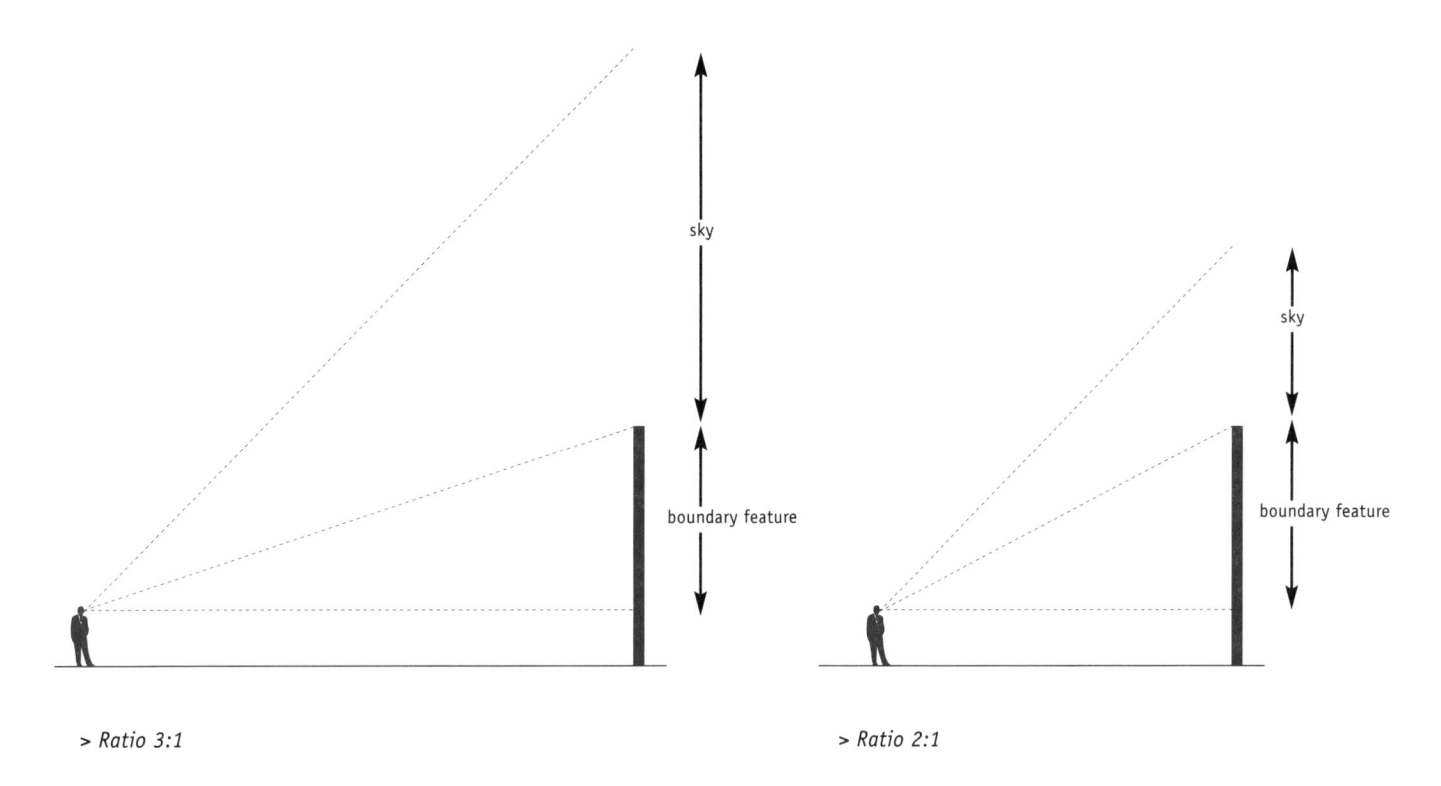

> Ratio 3:1

> Ratio 2:1

The greater the difference between distance and height becomes (e.g. ratio 8:1), the more strongly the sky will dominate the landscape architecture. And vice versa.

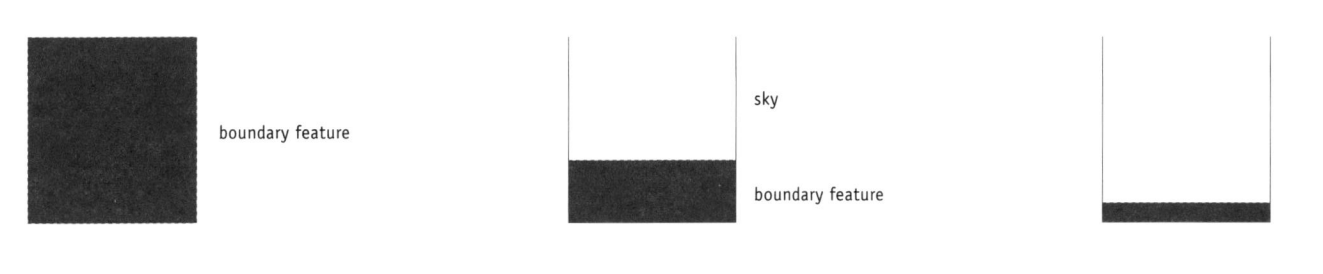

> Ratio 1:1 – no sky visible

> Ratio 3:1 – sky slightly dominant

> Ratio 8:1 – sky dominant

> **The human field of vision**

The human ability to see things, i.e. to know and to recognize them, is limited physiologically. If we do not move our eyes we can see in precise detail only within a very tight frame of about 1°. Within a field of approx. 30° to 36°, shapes are still relatively sharply discernible, and up to an angle of approx. 120° they become increasingly indistinct. Beyond this we can only make out movement (so-called "peripheral vision").

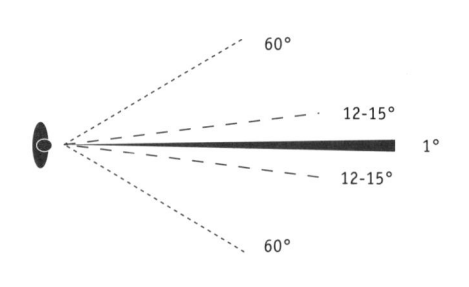

> Horizontal field of vision

> Vertical field of vision

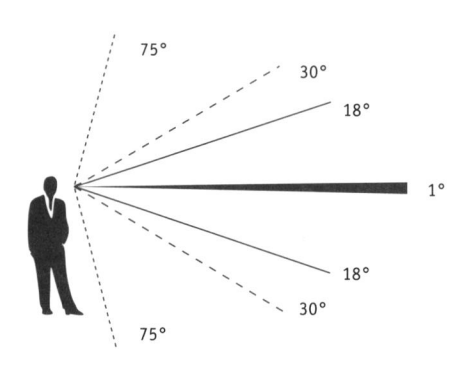

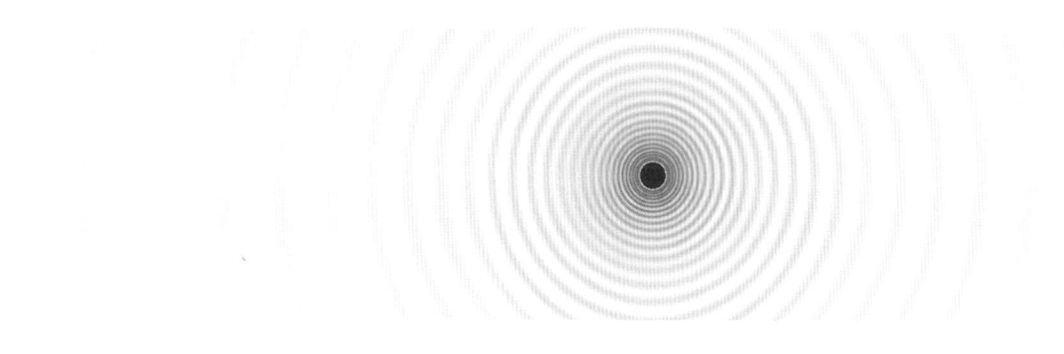

Ancient architects (e.g. Vitruvius) worked on an average value for the horizontal field of vision of 30° to 35°. At a distance of 10 m, this means a width of 6 m or a ratio of 5:3 (or 0.6: the harmonious ratio of the Great Sixth). The spatial proportions, in other words the ratio of length to width, of many ancient squares corresponds with this.

In the European sculptural tradition, empirical values relating to the human field of vision led to rules about the best point from which to look at a statue. Here a distinction was made between the ▬architectural-painterly viewpoint (ratio 3:1, corresponding to a angle of view approx. 18°), the ▬strictly architectural viewpoint (ratio 2:1, angle of view approx. 27°) and the ▬viewpoint for observing detail (ratio 1:1, angle of view 45°) [32].

[32] To prevent viewers from inadvertently going beyond the viewpoint for observing detail (distortion of forms), in many old monuments a hedge, a fence, a chain or a high step was placed at this point.

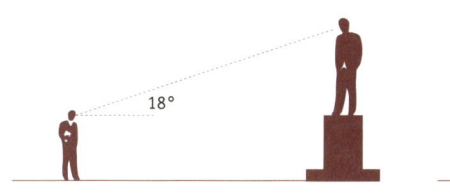

> *Architectural-painterly viewpoint*

> *Strictly architectural viewpoint*

> *Viewpoint for observing detail*

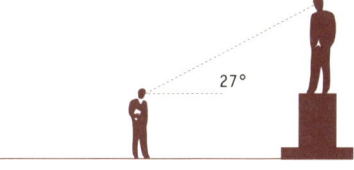

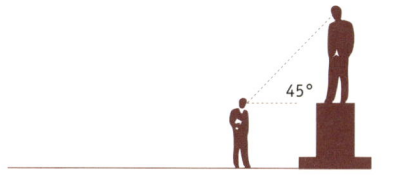

A ratio of 1:1 between the viewer and the boundary of the space is not to be generally recommended for public open spaces. As almost no sky can be seen at all, the dominant impression is of an insurmountable space (feeling of being cramped). But in contrast with this, the same ratio in the private sphere can evoke positive associations like feeling protected and secure. This can be desirable in small, private open spaces (atrium courtyards, conservatories etc.).

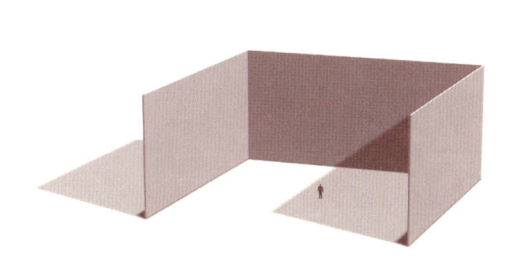

> *Ratio 1:1 (cramped/safe)*

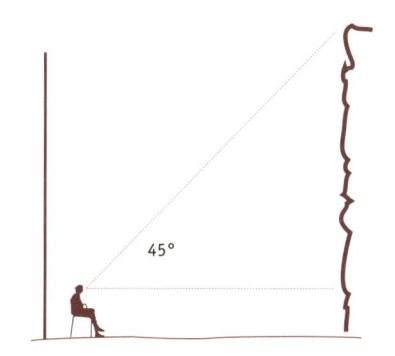

The ratio 1:1 should only be used if a sense of confinement and isolation is to be positively encouraged. If a situation of this kind is inevitable, because of existing buildings, old trees etc., the sense of being cramped can be reduced by **making the boundary less dominant** (reducing colour or brightness contrasts with the surroundings; extreme solution: mirror) **covering up the top of the boundary wall** (e.g. adding a light, low screen of trees in front of the boundary wall) **mediating intermediate level** (e.g. a pergola) **eye-catching features in the lower third of the boundary** (e.g. with "loud" planting, sculptures etc.) **reinforcing the area**, i.e. shifting the viewer's attention to the area (increasing its diversity e.g. by adding flowerbeds, different-coloured surface coverings etc.).

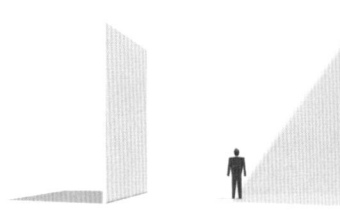

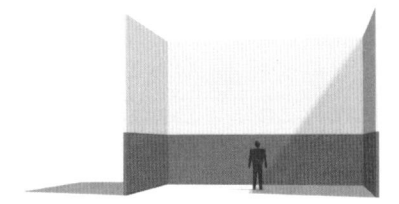

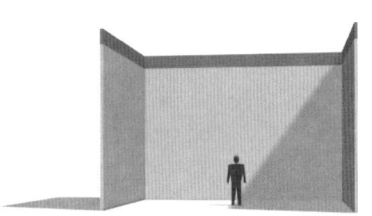

> *Ratio 1:1*

> *Making the boundary less dominant – space seems "more open"*

> *Strengthening the boundary – space seems "more cramped"*

> *Strengthening the base or weakening the top edge of the boundary – space seems "more open"*

> *Mediating intermediate height – pergola as an eye-catching feature in the central field of the boundary wall*

> *Emphasizing the top of the boundary – space seems "more cramped"*

> Reinforcing the area
(by drawing attention to it)

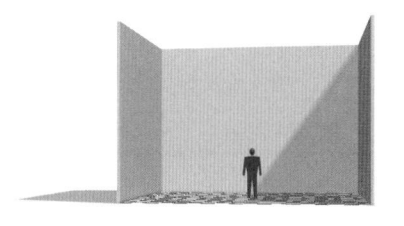

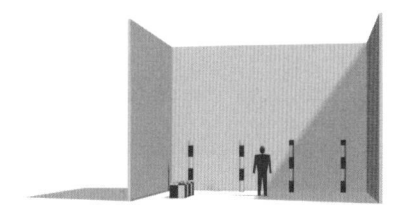

> Low, "loud" (special) items

> Expanding the space

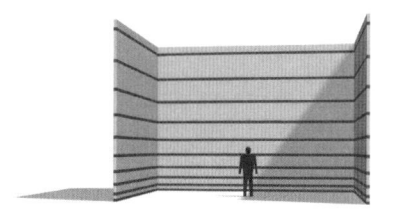

A space is often not experienced from the periphery, but roughly from the centre of the area. Even with a space ratio of 2:1 this produces a cramped 1:1 impression when standing in the middle. If this is undesirable, and the space cannot be enlarged to at least 3:1, then attractive focal points on the periphery (e.g. a little square, a bench) or at least a path through the space are a good idea, .

> Ratio 1:1 in the centre

> Peripheral path with a strong objective (door) – shifting of the viewpoint means: ratio 2:1

> Peripheral bench – ratio 2:1

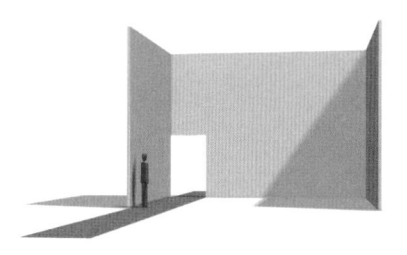

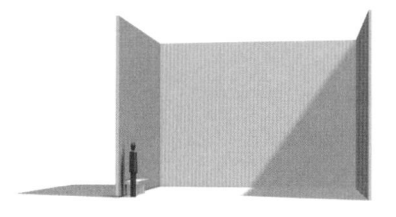

The ratio of ▬2:1 is recommended where a certain degree of seclusion and/or protection is sought, without feeling cramped. Important here: to guarantee seclusion, the boundaries must be solid to the ground (opaque, closed boundary wall).

The ratio of 2:1 is not suitable for undifferentiated open spaces that clearly emphasize the centre, as seeing the space from the centre shifts the ratio to 1:1, which is generally seen as cramping in open spaces.

> *Ratio 2:1 (seclusion)*

The ratio **_3:1** is the old scale for lawns in English landscape gardens. Lawns 100 - 120 metres long were bordered with size 1 trees (trees that reach a height of approx. 35 - 40 metres fully grown, like e.g. beech, lime, maple, oak ash etc.). The sky becomes a significant part of the field of vision, the space seems open and spacious from the periphery and protected and closed from the centre.

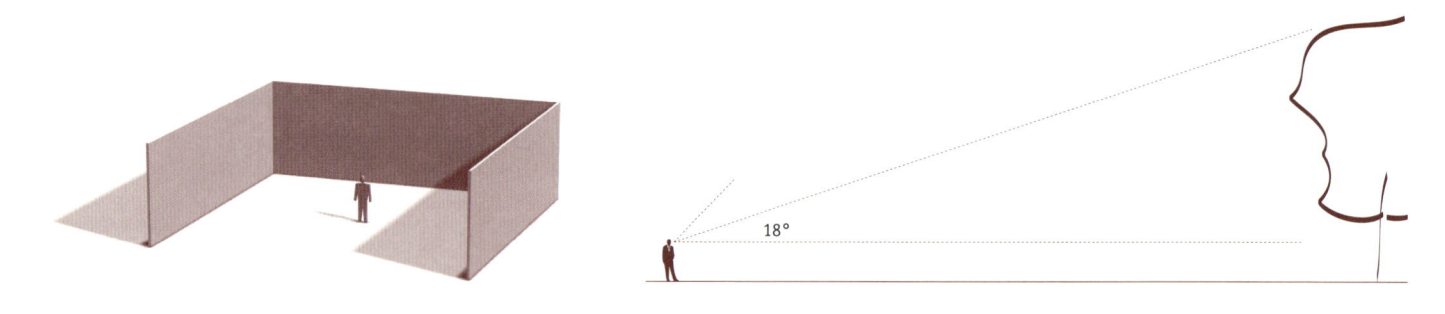

> *Ratio 3:1 (onset of openness)*

The ratios **_4:1 bis 6:1** create increasingly extensive, more open centres for their spaces, and very extensive peripheral situations, with a big sky creating a sense of distance.

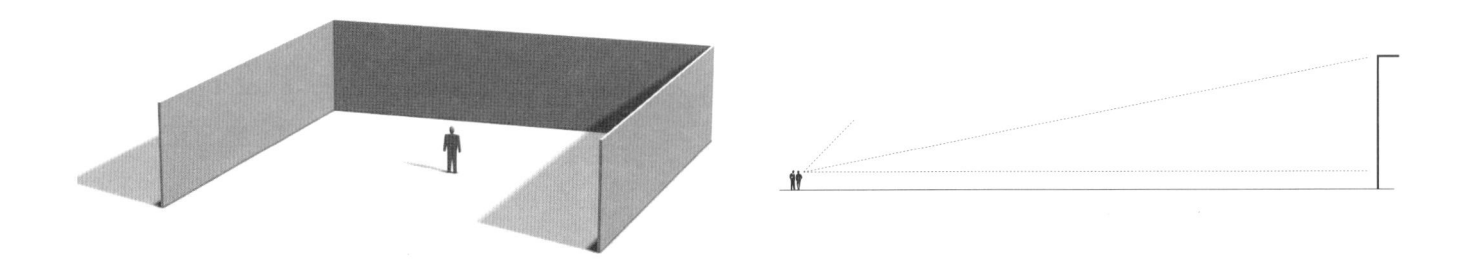

> Ration 4:1 (increasingly spacious)

If the major places intended for use (paths, squares etc.) are arranged correctly relative to the main direction of the space and the access features, then it is possible to achieve "spaciousness" within a relatively small area.

> Long narrow space – placing the areas in which most time is to be spent on the narrow sides can work against the feeling of being cramped

All ratios greater than this, in other words ▬**higher than 6:1**, seem more spacious and open, the feeling of being enclosed, a secure sense of space relating to the border, decreases considerably; this can lead to a feeling of being "lost under a huge sky", but also of freedom and lightness.

From a ratio of 6:1 onwards, clear starting-points, situative potentials **in** the area unit become more and more important and neces-

[33] Cf. p. 73: "Ratio 2:1". | sary [33]; the direct guiding function of openings, doorways etc, in the boundary walls decreases, and guidance by access (ways, paths, intermediate goals etc.) becomes important.

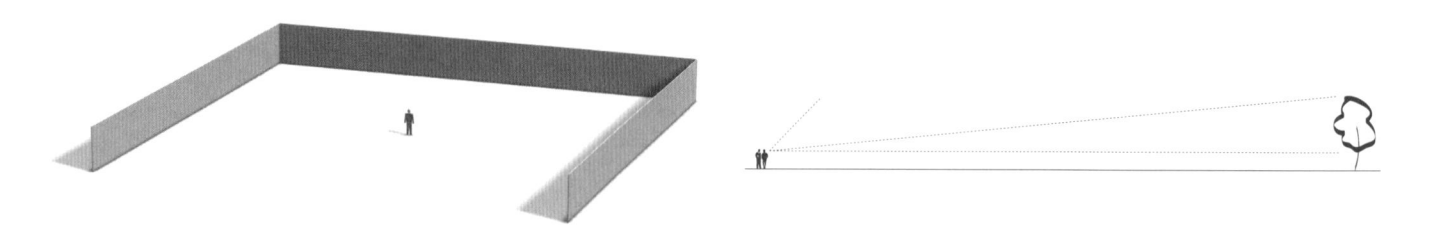

> *Ratio 10:1 "lost", "taking off", but also spaciousness, "freedom"*

> **Spatial effect and plants**

Plants used as boundaries change with time, they grow; their habit also changes when placed individually. So a garden that is spacious and open in the first few years after it is planted can change after 20-30 years into an uncomfortable, cramped "fortress". So when constructing tree spaces it is necessary to be familiar with the height specific to the species and the habit to be anticipated with changing times or in relation to position (solitary or tight group of trees).

Creating space with height differences

Differences in height have a great potential for creating space. Here the change of height, i.e. the transition from one level to another, forms the boundary. Height differences can be created by an abrupt clear change **(terracing)** or as a gradual transition without an independent, clearly defined transitional area **(modelling)**. Terracing is represented on a plan by embankment lines, while modelled land is shown by contours.

Terracing characteristically shows a clear division between almost horizontal areas (terraced spaces) and independent, more or less steeply sloping areas (terrace embankments; in extreme cases: terrace walls).

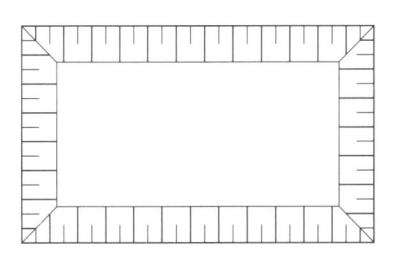

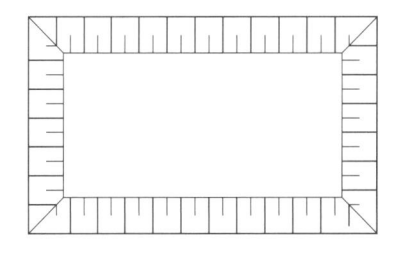

> *Terraced, "hard" hollow*

> *Terraced, "free" hollow*

> *Terraced, "free" plateau*

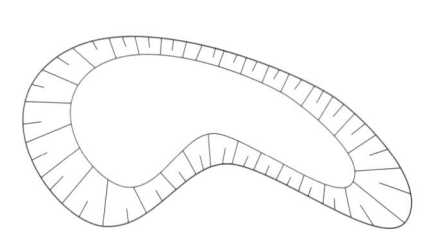

The more indistinct and shallow the transition between levels of differing height becomes, the more important it is for the area to have a characteristic form if space is to be created [34].

[34] Cf. p. 50-51: "The weaker the boundary, the stronger the area (and vice versa)".

> Terrace wall – not an independent boundary area, but a clear edge in the space

> Steep terrace edge – narrow boundary area, clear edge in the space

> Shallow terrace edge – broad area with use-quality, but weak spatial effect

On slopes, terracing is achieved by cutting into the site, adding material, or both.

> Terrace (incised)

> Terrace (added)

> Terrace (combination)

If the area distinct from the surrounding incline is not more or less horizontal, but just clearly shallower than the general slope, it is not called a terrace but a **shoulder**.

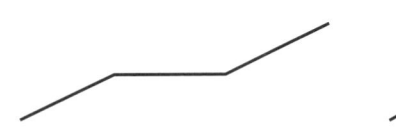

> Terraces – horizontal plan on the slope

> Shoulder – shallower sloping level on the steeper slope

Unlike terracing, modelling means a "soft", rounded form for the height difference. Characteristic features of modelling are ▪ the lack of a clear borderline between shallow and steep sections of the terrain ▪ the form of a sinus curve in cross-section ⌒ i.e. a shallow beginning or end and a steep central section [35] ▪ a constantly changing incline.

[35] Almost all familiar landscape shapes of the "natural" medium relief have such a form caused by the "modelling" force of streaming water and/or wind.

> *Steep embankment*

> *Shallow embankment*

> *Banked hill (plan)*

> *Banked hill (section)*

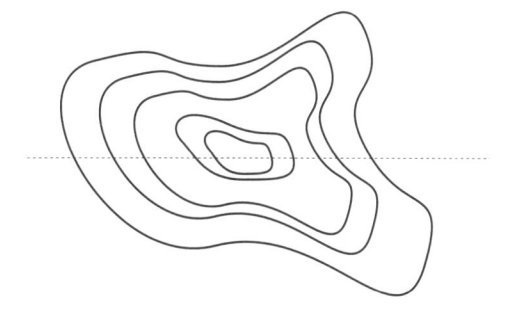

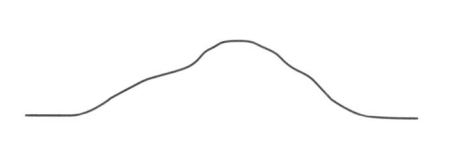

▬ Height differences and spatial effect

Whether height differences make a clear effect or not depends on the interplay between the height of the rise or fall in the terrain and the observer's stand- and viewpoint ("human scale").

Raising an area relative to its surroundings "enhances" its meaning. Up to a height of about 150 cm (easy for adults to look over) gives the rise a sense of extroversion, a relative sense of belonging and openness. Rises of over 150 cm gradually shift the effect to isolation and privacy.

Even ▬ rises of 30-50 cm give areas spatial independence, indicating a differentiating, different use potential; but the idea of linking up with, belonging to the surroundings predominates strongly.

> *Raising the height by 30-50 cm*

▬ Raising the level by 70 cm (up to 100 cm) – especially when the surface materials and textures are similar or the same – leads to a (delicate) balance between an impression of dividing or of bringing together. The raised area acquires a spatial independence changing with the difference in height, but without (at least for an adult who is standing up) seeming isolated from the surroundings. There is already a strong sense of division for children but also for people who are sitting.

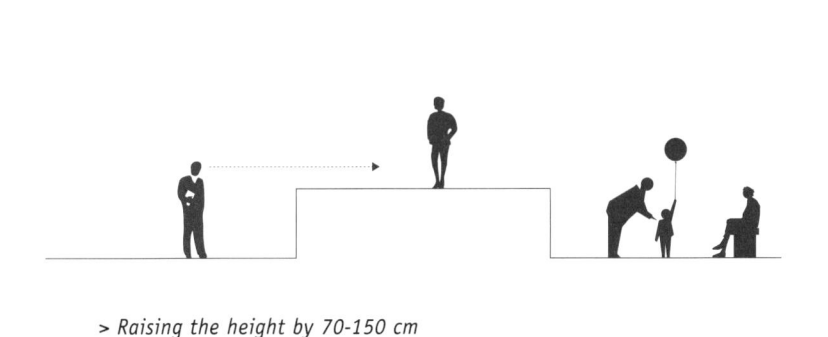

> *Raising the height by 70-150 cm*

▬ Further raising the height creates a strong sense of spatial separation (closed boundary wall from below, little need to make contact from above). Different uses without taking any notice of each other are possible in both "spaces".

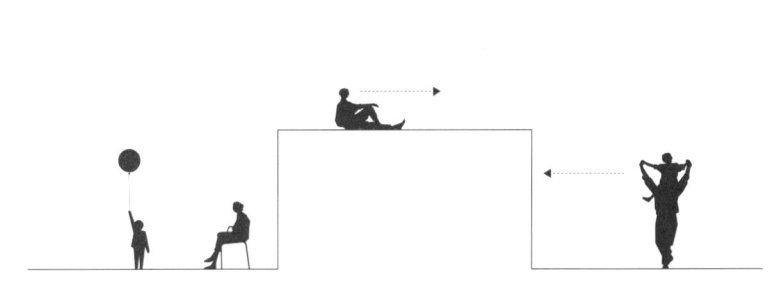

> *Raising the height more than 150-160 cm*

Lowered or sunken areas create spaces that tend to feel isolated; they can also indicate that the potential uses demand a certain degree of protection (children playing, display herbaceous border etc.).

_Lowering the terrain by approx. 100 (max. 150) cm conveys seclusion, but the linking element between above and below usually remains defining.

_Lowering the ground by over 150 cm rapidly removes the connection between the upper and lower sections. The feeling of security increasingly becomes one of discomfort, being shut in, in case of free eye contact even to unprotected exposure.

> Lowering the height by 30-50 cm
(sense of connection predominant)

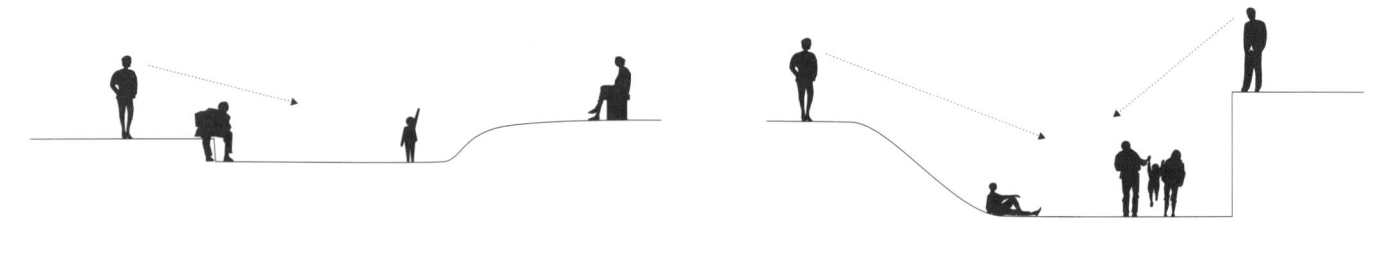

> Clearly lowering the height by over 150 cm – the sense of separation predominates despite free eye contact

▬ **Planting to achieve visual changes of relief**

Additional planting can make small and medium relief situations look different spatially. _**Embankments** can be raised or lowered visually by terraced planting (using habit appropriate species).

> Existing bank

> Raised bank

> Flattened bank

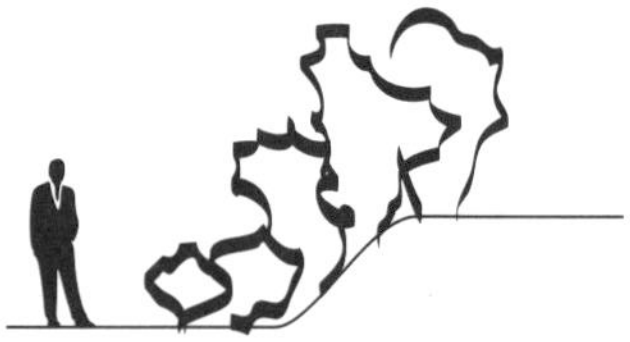

Something similar applies to _ **hills**: planting can emphasize or weaken the relief form.

Planting tall or semi-tall trees on the **hilltop** makes the hill look more mobile and "airy"; it is possible to look through under the trees, which means the actual relief shape is retained.

But closed vegetation groups following the shape of the hill (e.g. with several layers of trees and shrubs) raise the overall relief, blend into the hill and make it look "higher" and "heavier". The actual relief of the hill is scarcely discernible any longer.

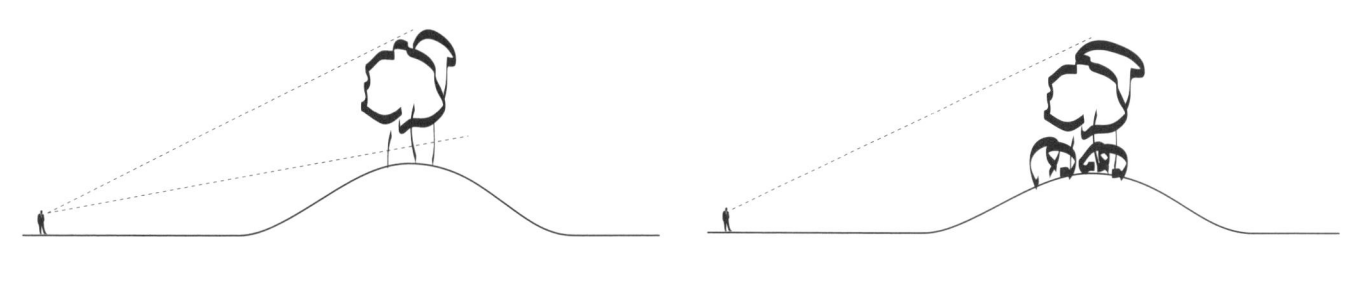

> *Heightening – the relief of the hill can still be made out*

> *Heightening – relief of the hill indistinct*

Planting on hillsides makes the relief less intelligible, planting **in front of** the hill flattens the relief. This makes the hill itself insignificant.

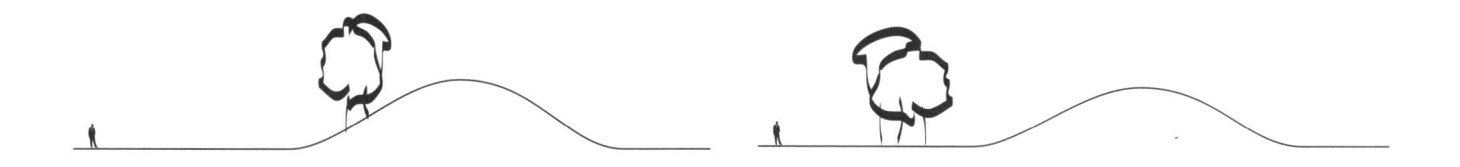

> *Planting the hillside – neither emphasis or weakening unclear relief.*

> *Planting in front of the hill – hill visually flattened*

**Shallow dips** can be reinforced by height-staggered planting at the edges. These raised sections give the dip a clear, highly independent spatial setting.

> Slight dip

> Raised edges – dip stronger

**Steep garden slopes** can be flattened visually by planting taller plants (offering an open view at ground level) on the valley side and lower (dense) plants on the upper side. If the higher elements are on the top side, the effect is reversed and the slope "is" steeper.

> Slope – made shallower visually by planting

> Slope – made steeper visually by planting

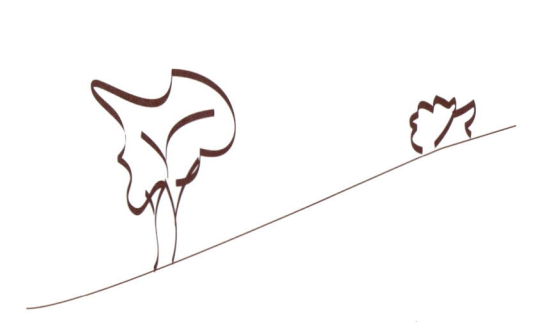

The grove

The copse or ancient grove, trees grouped densely relative to the surroundings, is an independent spatial type. Groves are "houses": the unity of area and the border elements emerge almost as a reversal of the usual spaces created by landscape architecture [36]. The crowns of the trees create a darker, roofed and more protected space in comparison with the light, open surroundings that are constitutive for a grove.

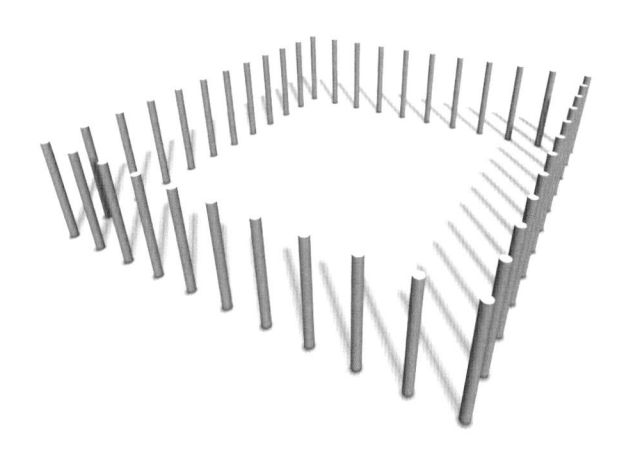

[36] Cf. p. 48: "Landscape architectural spaces".

> *Space – vertical boundaries, sky open*

> *Grove – closed (roof)*

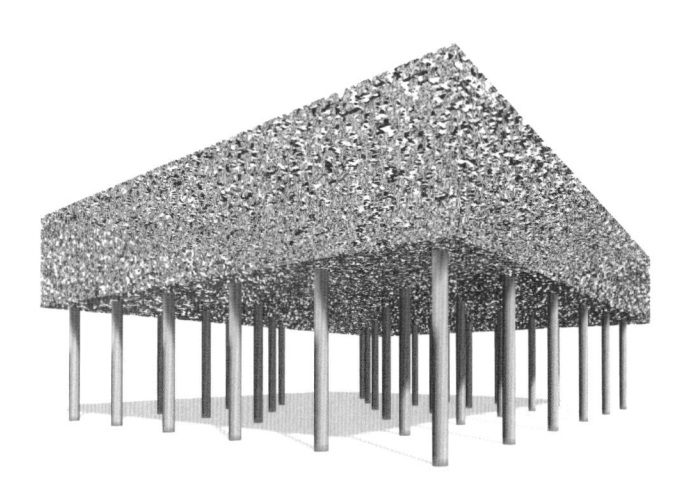

Groves can have different characters, different moods. This depends above all on the choice of tree species (light, light-permeable to shady, dark trees, light-green sun-flecked to "heavy" dark-green shadows, shiny or matt foliage etc.) but also on the density of the tree positioning and the planting structure (severe/formal or free/irregular grove).

> *Formal grove – precise, reliable, "tidy", calm, "stiff"*

> *Free grove – playful, promising freedom, restless, "heavenly"; the uniform sense of space is mixed with an increasing sense of breaking up*

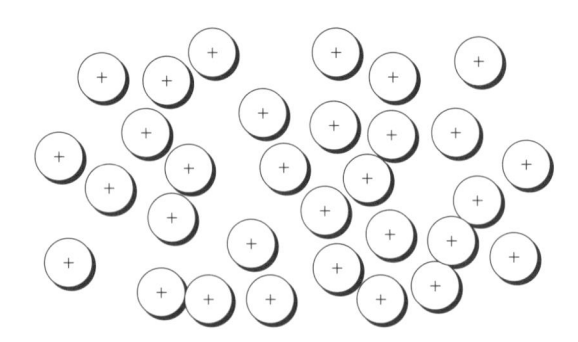

_**Formal groves** form a regular tree-roof, thus defining (dependent on the location) darker, shadier (mysterious) areas; they can be loosely closed, and seem shady and comfortable (wandering patches of sun on the ground) or, if the trees are arranged less tightly, bright, light and invitingly transparent.

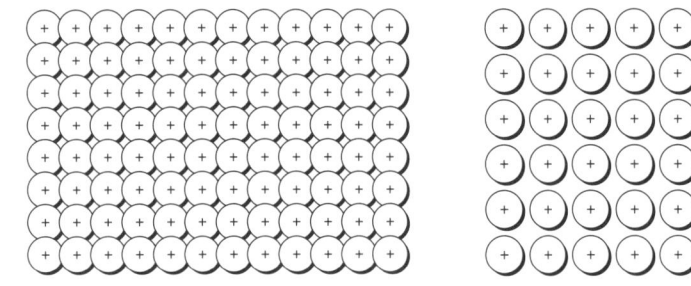

> *Grove, dense and closed*

> *Grove, loosely closed*

> *Grove, loose*

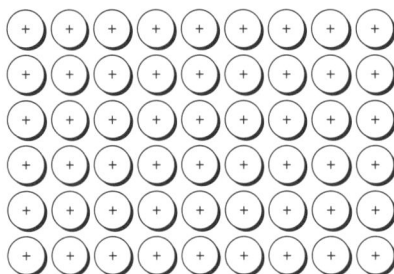

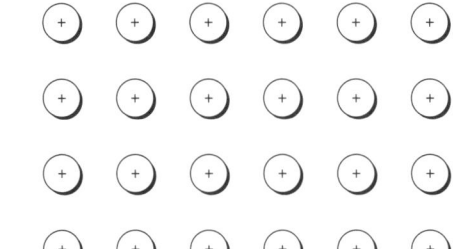

If formal groves are broken up into groups, this creates a new spatial situation inside the grove (clearings). The breaking up can be strict and regular, or attractive contrasts with the regularity of the grove grid can be created by irregular gaps and groups.

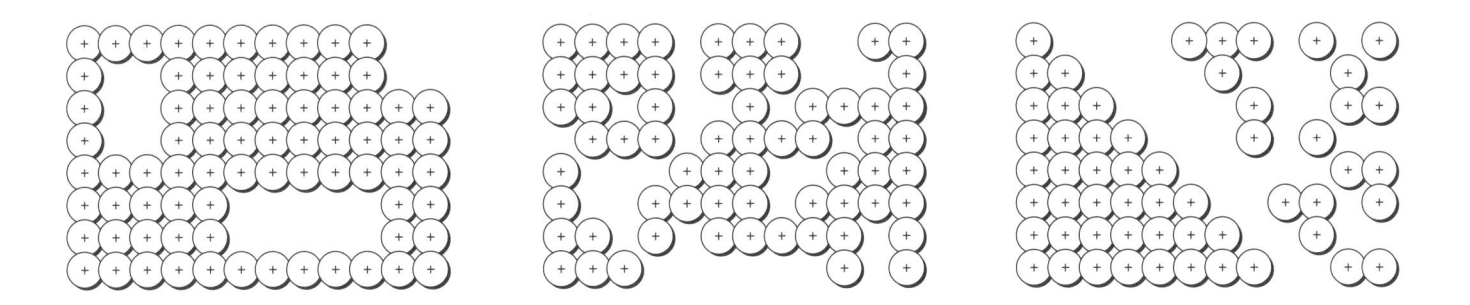

> Regular, formal clearings on a strict grid

> Free clearings on a strict grid

> Freer clearing emphasizing direction

Free, "natural" groves, unlike formal groves are not based on a regular grid. The distances between the trees and the sequences of light and shady areas are irregular; greater gaps alternate with small, dense and dark areas. Thus groves can create a very wide range of moods: anything from arcadian to melancholic, according to the tree species.

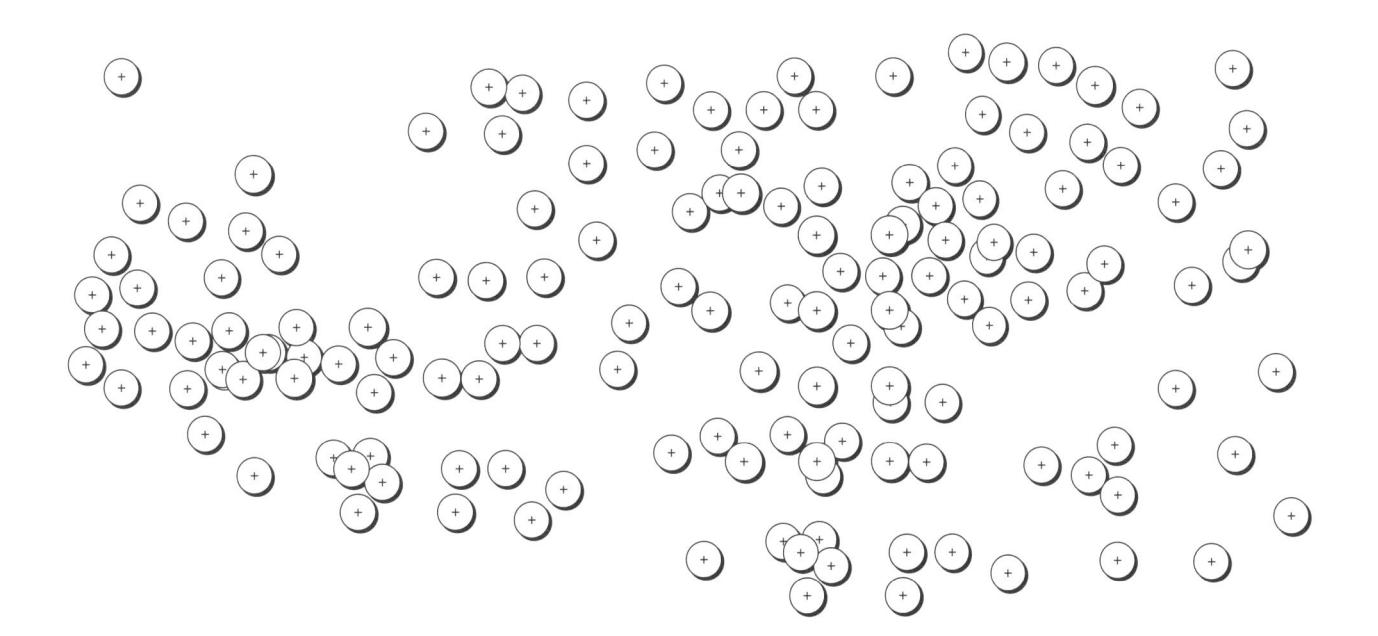

ideas

88

quotations

sketches

questions

additions

3.2 Creating focal points ("place")

Any design intervention enters into a dialogue with what is already there: a dot on a white sheet of paper draws attention to itself, is a focal point in that context: as viewers we involuntarily relate the position of this point to the edges of the sheet.

The same applies to open space: every special point, every intervention is intelligible only in connection with the spatial conditions.

Focal points are created on the basis of their special position or their special character within the context.

Focal point

The fact that people look for connections all the time, categorize phenomena, "relate" them to each other is important for focal points as well: focal points identify special, extraordinary areas within a certain spatial context. In comparison to space, as an independent (if need be self-sufficient) phenomenon, focal points cannot be understood out of context. Their effect, their character, their "fate" is inseparably linked with the spatial peculiarities that surround them. But: they do influence these as well.

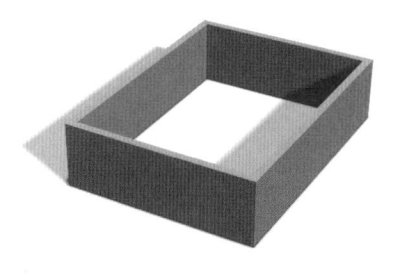

> *Space – "introverted" (autonomous)*

> *Focal point – "extrovert" – needs external reference points (or creates a "spatial bell" gradually becoming thinner the greater the distance from the focal point is)*

> *Space and focal point*

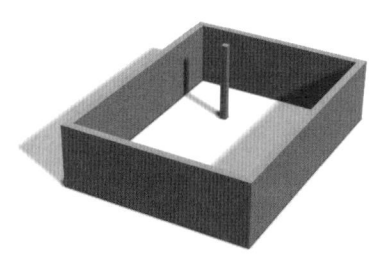

Focal points strengthen, change or create spatial situations. They define areas, condense meanings, attract attention, are "attractors" [37]. Focal points are anchorage and orientation points for our movement, our looks, our behaviour. At the same time they refer to (new) contexts, motivating and reflecting links between different shapes in the space.

[37] The concept of the attractor comes from non-linear dynamics: they are shapes "that seem to attract the system's condition of movement, that are attractive." Cf. www.nld.physik.uni-mainz.de

Spaces derive their natures from places. Martin Heidegger

One characteristic of focal points is that they can be described comparatively: they are larger, smaller, lighter, darker, rounder, more angular, bluer, greener, damper, softer, more interesting, more exciting, more boring, longer, fuller, straighter, more extravagant, shriller, calmer, more unpleasant, clearer, emptier, fuller etc. than the surroundings.

> **Some examples of focal points**

> Density in emptiness

> Emptiness in density

> Disorder in order

> Texture in structure

> Rounded within angular shapes

> Beginning/end of directions

> Interruption of the continuous

> Opening up something closed

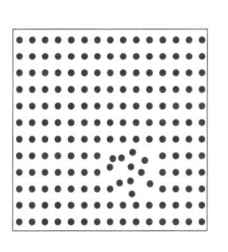

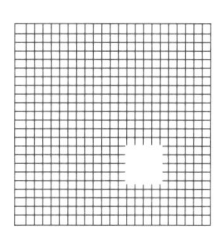

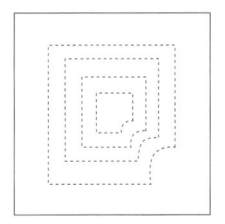

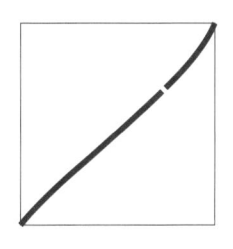

▬ Special position

Focal points are extraordinary in relation to their immediate vicinity. In this respect, their special qualities can be derived "automatically" (on the basis of simple geometrical positional references) from the form of the space or from the boundaries (e.g. the centre of a flat, uniform surface, lines parallel with the boundaries, ideal extensions of strong directional links etc.).

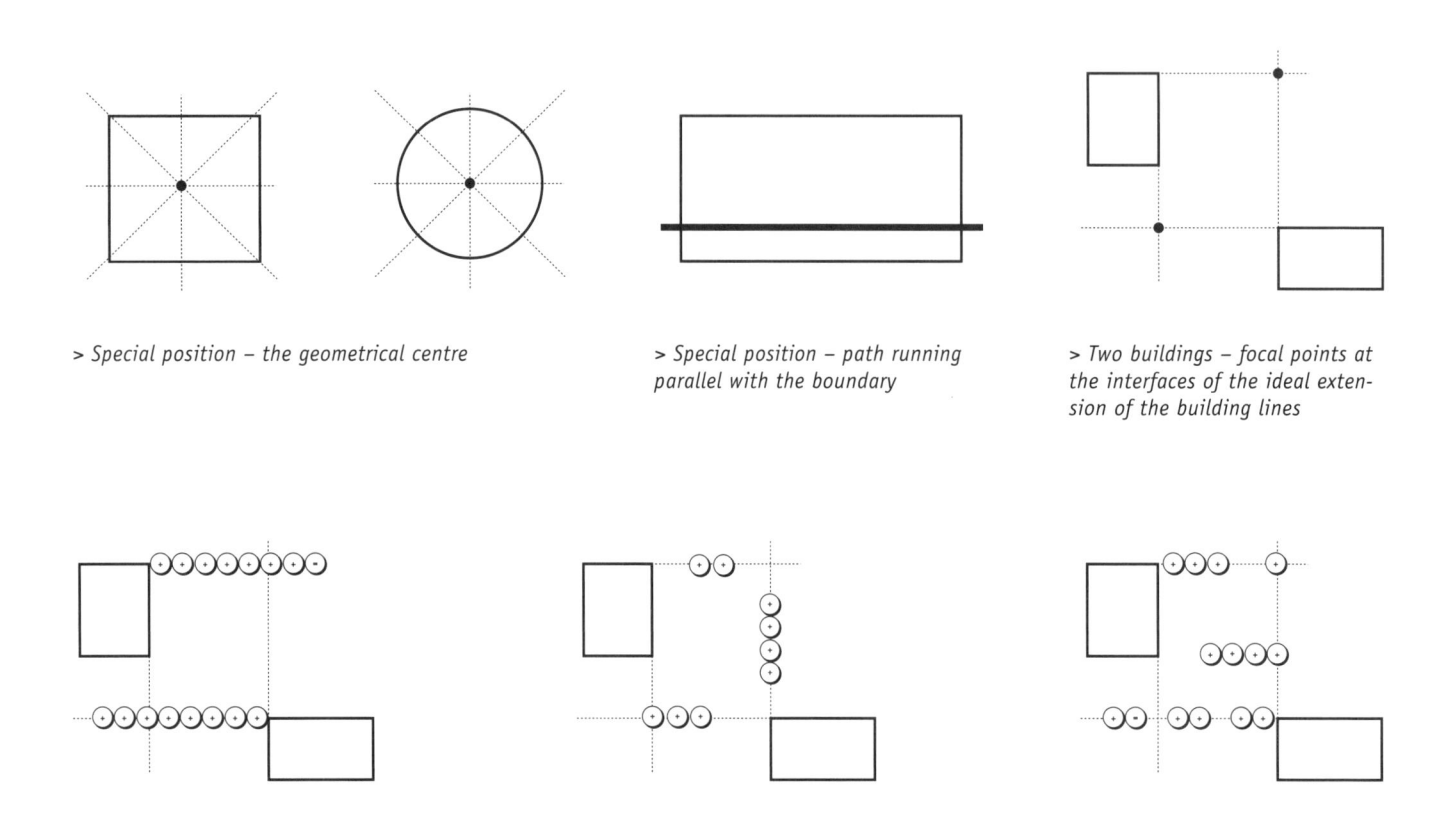

> *Special position – the geometrical centre*

> *Special position – path running parallel with the boundary*

> *Two buildings – focal points at the interfaces of the ideal extension of the building lines*

> *Two buildings – trees placed on special lines*

In the same way, a special situation can arise from special morphological qualities. In open terrain these are above all exposed places that are clearly distinct from their surroundings like hilltops, flat areas on a steep slope, particular relief lines (slope edges, foot lines, ridge lines), river beds etc.

> *Special position – hilltop*   > *Special position – terrace on slope*   > *Special line – terrace edge*

Design interventions that address special positions seem calm, integrated and natural, as a rule they need only minimal additional identification; they emphasize and strengthen what is already there.

> The straight line and the right angle

The right angle is not called "right" for nothing. With the straight line, it has represented the cultural response to mobile, dangerous and unpredictable nature, human work in the wilderness, from the dawn of human civilization. Both the right angle and the straight line stand for "human work", for predictability, certainty and familiarity. Where it does not exist really and materially, it is sought and recognized via ideal lines of reference.

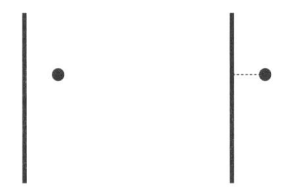

> Point and vertical line – the ideal reference line adopts the right angle (shortest distance)

> Point and tilted line – <1> the ideal reference line adopts the right angle (shortest distance). But: <2> Because of the predominantly horizontal structure of the lines of text on this page (= context), there is also a pull towards a horizontal reference line

A right angle is created when two straight lines meet in such a way that the directions indicated are neutralized: the different movements are in a state of equilibrium. For this reason the right angle is the calmest way different directions can meet. In contrast with this, two lines meeting outside the right angle lead to unrest, instability, but also to movement and dynamics.

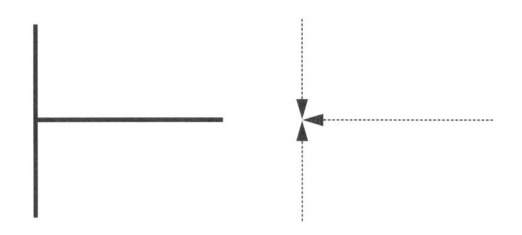

> Line connection at right angles – neutralizing the directions; calm, reconciled situation

> Line connection not at right angles – new direction resulting from this; unrest, but dynamics as well

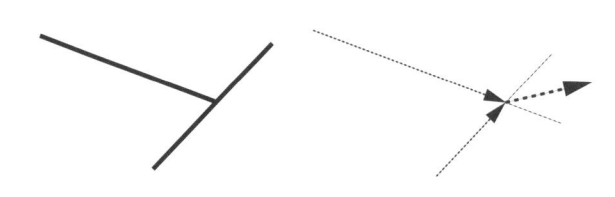

▬ Emphasized (designed) focal points

Focal points that lie outside the force fields defined by the geometrical or morphological conditions and that are intended to be relevant within the design need a clear, solidly material presence. This applies all the more strongly the further their position or the point from which they are viewed is from "automatically effective" focal points (e.g. geometrical centre).

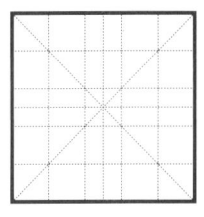

> Square plan with special positions derived from the boundaries

> Marking the centre – the calmest position, as all areas are of equal value

> Marking the central horizontal symmetrical axis – calm as it is parallel with the boundary lines; indeterminate (disturbing, shifting) because it is close to the geometrical focus (mutual competition)

> Marking the diagonal symmetrical axis – clear differentiation between "contained" and "open" area, strong link with the left-hand, upper part of the space

> Marking clearly off centre – very strong link with the left-hand boundary, but still the focal point in the space

> Marking the corner – strong weighting for the area but no longer a focus in the space (strengthening the border rather than the space)

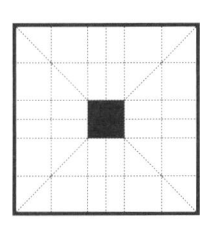

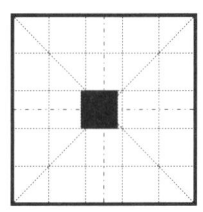

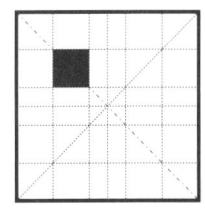

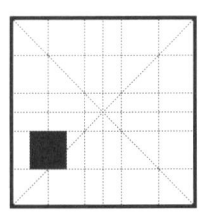

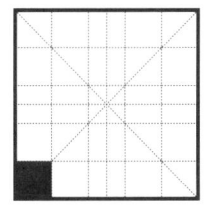

As long as the position of a focal point is still clearly and recognizably derived from the context (through direction and position), it confirms (emphasizes) the context it relates to, categorizes itself, "subjects" itself to the contextual requirements. A connection is sought, the independence of the space as a whole is reinforced.

Focal points desirable in design terms whose position cannot be derived from existing borders and reference lines are more striking, but tend to be disturbing; to understand their position (within the space) one has to reflect more intensely. When focal points and lines are deliberately "pulled out" of the dominant, self-explanatory positional and directional links, then the independence of the space is impaired in favour of the focal points (or lines) themselves. They can refer at the same time to ideal ordering systems and relations outside the given spatial situation.

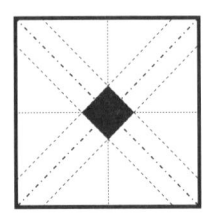

> 45° – turn in central position – still tied into the positional relationships within the space calmly by the diagonals (right angle!)

> Turn – introduction of a new direction; still relatively calm because of the central position

> Turn and positional shift. The lower, right-hand area becomes crucial to the space as a whole; the space is weakened in favour of the focal point

> Very independent focal points – significant "weakening" of the space (of the boundaries), reference to links outside the space

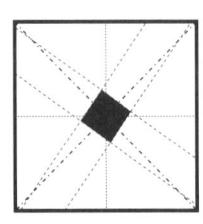

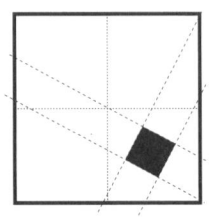

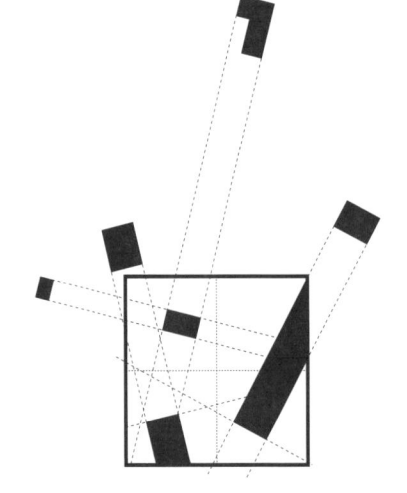

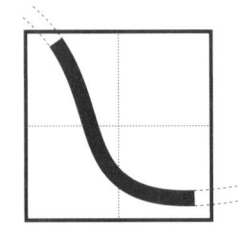

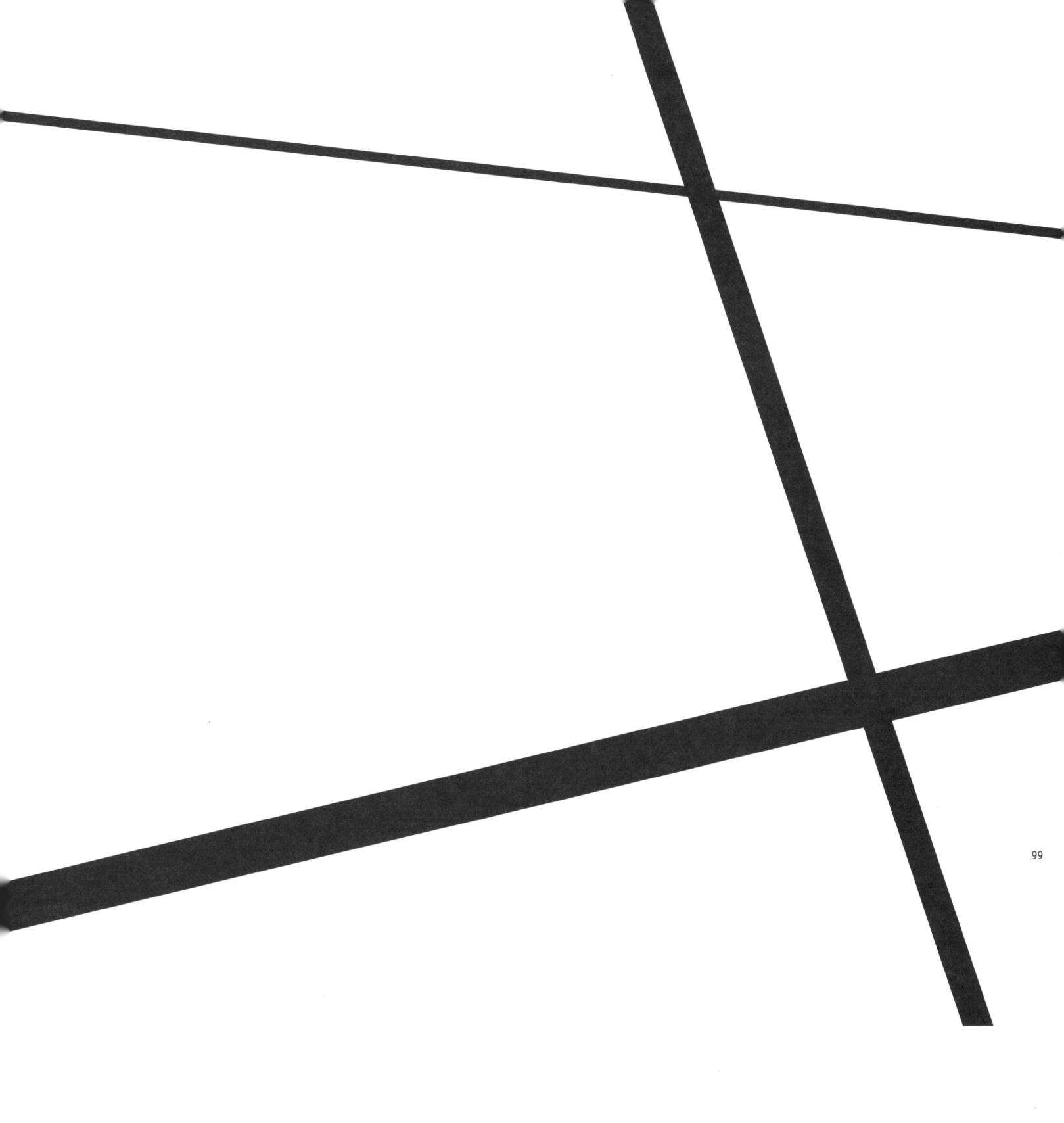

notes

ideas

quotations

sketches

questions

additions

3.3 Movement and access ("path")

The ways of man are not unfathomable.

The way we move forward, keep on in the same direction or turn aside, slow down our pace or speed up, is predictable to a large extent.

The quality of access is decided by the designer's ability to support forward movement, effectively anticipating it by design measures ("positive guidance").

Landscape architecture means accompanying movement gently.

▬ Movement – motive and reaction

Where we are going, and how quickly, depends on our motive for moving and our reaction to the surroundings. The motive (why am I going?) plays a key role here: do we want to get somewhere quickly (like an underground station) or do we want to saunter, stroll, jog, dawdle etc.?

Our reaction to the surroundings (how and where am I going?) is based on our ability (our necessity) to recognize (to look for) forms, in other words characteristic links between features of the surroundings. This basic need, this reaction to specific morphological factors affects our progress in characteristic ways. Two (very ancient) elements are crucial to this kind of movement: the need for ▬**anticipatory orientation** and that for proceeding as ▬**"inattentively"** as possible.

▬ Anticipatory orientation

Paths indicate connection. As natural lines, largely comprehensible over a long distance, they stand for certainty (about direction), familiarity and predictability. Paths mark customary, frequent lines of movement, they best satisfy people's need for anticipatory orientation. If there is no actual path available to indicate a line that can be followed "with certainty", then we instinctively look for points we can relate to ("way-markers") in the terrain that help us to "form" and predict our own movement lines.

Path markers are clear forms, recognizable from a distance (I recognize – I know – therefore I'm on the right track) as reference points to help us to move forward. As well as path markers at particular points (striking individual trees, rock formations, buildings etc.) ▬special lines in the terrain relief (linear markers like small ridges, shorelines, little valleys etc.) are used consciously or instinctively as important aids to progress. They make it possible, like an existing way or path, to move forward confidently over long stretches.

For example, terraces and hills (so long as they do not clearly lie across the desired direction of movement) are followed for preference along the bottom of a slope or the top of a terrace, or over the top (of a low hill). These lines function as linear way-markers, as they are special because they seldom occur within the topography.

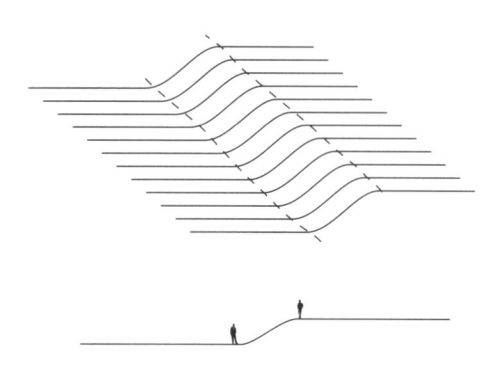

> *Special relief lines (terrace, plateau) – lower and upper edge*

> *Special relief lines (hill) – foot lines, ridge lines*

Proceeding "inattentively"

Proceeding "inattentively" means instinctively looking for a way of proceeding and maintaining an even stride that needs as little attention as possible, saves energy and is comfortable. So we should have to pay minimal attention to the path itself (i.e. to its surface in relation to where we put our foot down next). It is only when we do not have to concentrate on every single step [38] that we are able to turn our attention to other phenomena along the way (e.g. the beautiful view, the next way-marker, the deer at the edge of the wood etc.) [39].

[38] Cf. p. 18: "Superization".
[39] Probably originally also to be able to respond to potential danger quickly. (Cf. also animal behaviour studies).

A lake. High hills all around. It is hot, summer. He wants to go for a swim. He leaves the tranquil mooring with bare feet, and picks his way precariously across the steep rocks to the shore. First contact with the cold water. Slowly, with his gaze fixed on his feet, he makes his way over the sharp pebbles.

How much attention can he be paying to his breath-taking surroundings?

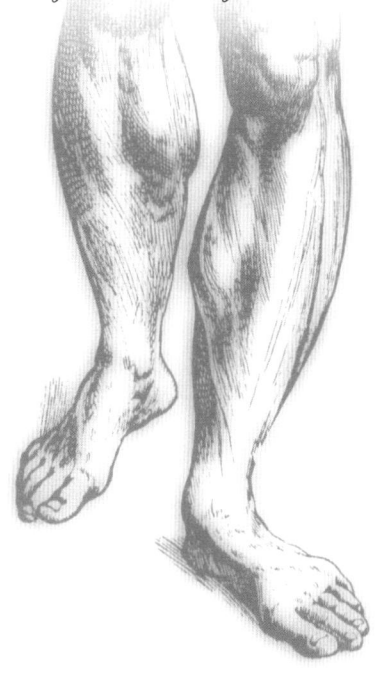

The fact that people want to move forward evenly, feeling relaxed, "inattentively" can be seen clearly from some typical human behaviours when on the move: ▪ On flat terrain that can be walked across at an even pace, an almost straight line is taken between starting-point and destination.

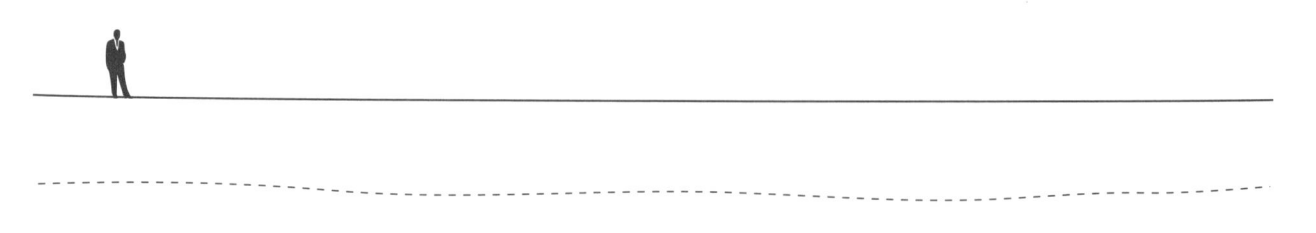

> Straight walk on even terrain that can be traversed at an even pace

▪ If the line we are trying to move along is interrupted we have to abandon it to go round the obstacle and then return to moving in the original direction. This obviously applies to large objects (houses, cliffs, trees), but also to disturbances of the small-scale relief, rocks, clumps of tall grass, a wet patch etc. Such diversions rarely involve abrupt changes of direction, but shallow (predictable) curves.

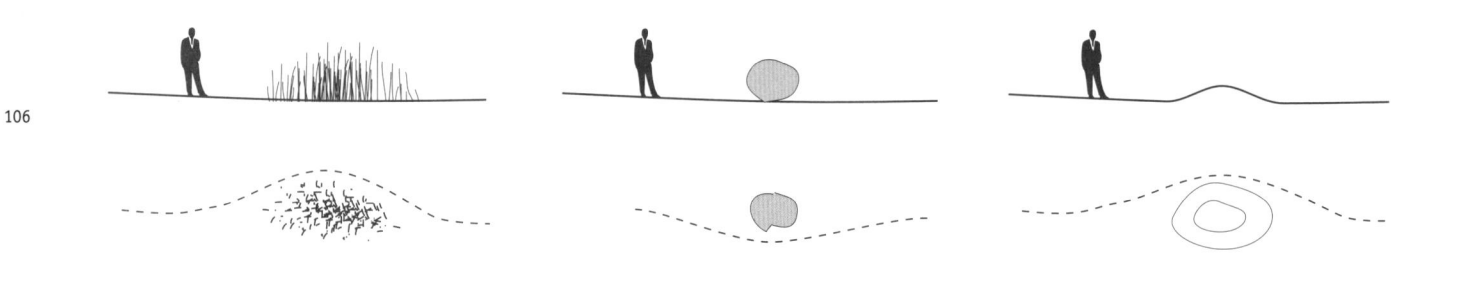

> Going round an area of long grass

> Going round a rock

> Going round a slight rise in the terrain

■ People tend to make a detour round height differences that run across the main line of movement. If this is not possible, a line is chosen that avoids frequent changes of incline (a line that goes up- or downhill evenly). Here, given a similar incline, hollows are seen as less of an obstacle than hills. (Perhaps because in the case of a dip the direction taken and the qualities of the surface can still be made out, while on a hill there is a period when neither the destination nor the route can still be made out.)

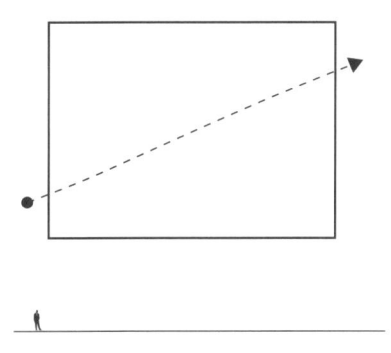

> Even terrain – crossed in a straight line

> Steep hill – crossed around the side (short, even ascent – level stretch along a contour – even descent)

> Shallow dip (low hill) – crossed almost directly along a line with an even incline

> Steep dip – crossed around the sides with a slight, even incline in the upper part of the slope

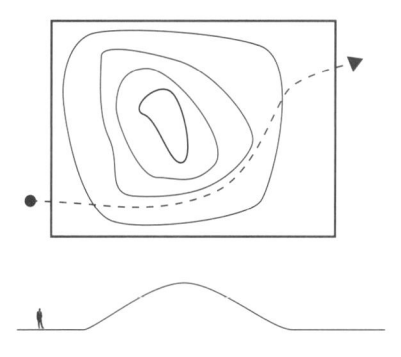

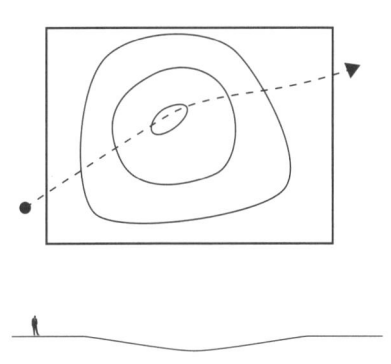

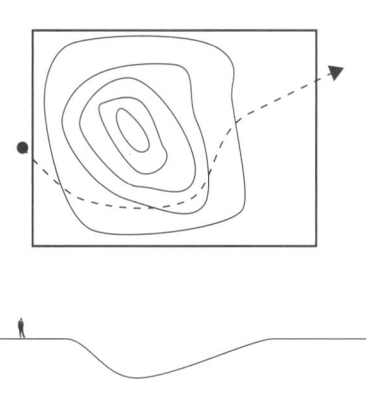

▬ To avoid uncomfortable walking "off-balance" (surface not at right angles to the axis of the body), people instinctively look for

[40] Cf. pp. 77-78: Terracing and shoulder. | shoulders in hilly terrain [40].

> *Banking so that the surface can be walked on at right angles to the body axis (this is how all paths are built!)*

> *Shoulder*

▬ Short, manageable steep points are climbed directly (on the contour gradient) if there is no more pleasant route (shoulder). For longer steep stretches a less energetic climb diagonal to the slope is preferred. Here there tends to be a change of direction, frequently after similar distances ("kick turns" to confirm direction and get one's breath). The steeper the slope, the shorter the distance between the individual changes of direction.

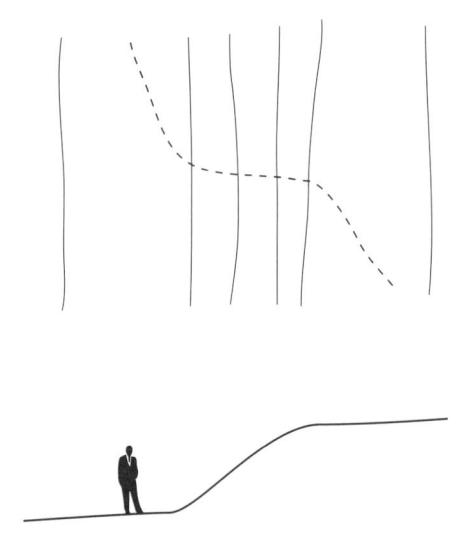

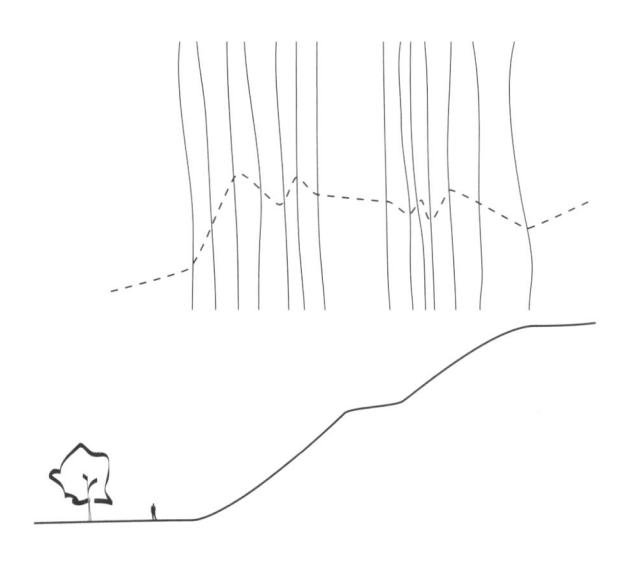

> *Small change of height – traversed rapidly and evenly on the contour gradient*

> *Longer slopes – even ascent diagonal to the slope*

> **"Beaten" track – the archetypal path**

Frequent passage along a certain line in the terrain creates the archetype of the path, the trampled or beaten track. Using an available beaten track, in other words one that has already been frequently walked along, is one of the most important reasons of all for choosing the line we walk along ("man is a gregarious animal", "successor syndrome").

> Grass

> Line walked along; lower, compressed, lack of vegetation or typical "trample-resistant" vegetation

> Consolidation of the beaten track; taller vegetation on the edge of the path

▬ Positive control

Being aware of how people behave instinctively when walking is one of the keys to designing landscape architecture. Even the most beautifully designed route for a path will not be accepted by users if it runs counter to these criteria. The consequences can be seen even a short time after a project opens to the public: sections that were planned as discrete areas are trampled over and paths formed, planned paths are deserted. This also reduces the pleasure derived from areas that are attractive precisely because people don't walk through them (rest areas, grass for playing on etc.). Frequently, retrospective attempts are made to respond to paths created spontaneously like this by erecting barriers, fences or prohibitive signs ("negative control"). But even measures like this do not usually have any chance of lasting success (hedges are trampled down, fences broken etc.).

Positive control means anticipating users' paths as a matter of course or gently "manipulating" them, it means enticing rather than forbidding.

Any good access programme is based on **analysing goals**: existing destinations (or some that have to be retained) have to be assessed, and those that have to be created within an open space located; **visual links** and **path signs** are "positive control" devices.

_**Visual links** help to motivate forward movement. Making attractive intermediate goals available (linked views, interesting places etc.) can provide additional motivation for moving along a path and/or trigger natural, "enticing" changes of direction.

_**Path signs** clarify the line of a path. They are uniform in terms of surface (material quality), path profile (small-scale relief), path width and markers accompanying the path (e.g. relief, individual features – classically: tree by the path).

▬ External and internal access

External access deals with getting to an open space and the main entrance points to it from the surrounding area (roads, public transport, important buildings, exits and ways across etc.). Normally landscape architects can influence this only to a limited extent, as it is much more subject to non-local (expert) planning authorities. Quality criteria for external access to open spaces include targeted routes (preferably car-free), simple orientation and clear entrance points.

Internal access starts where external access ends: at the entrances. It is the generic term for all the structures and elements aimed primarily at movement in an open-air complex.

▬ Problems/aims of internal access

Access is rarely an end in itself [41]. In fact it should operate like a pleasant companion, prescribing which direction to move in as if it were matter of course, showing visitors where to look and making it possible for users to pay attention to other things.

[41] Exception: formal gardens (e.g. Baroque flowerbeds).

**Access means creating areas.** The linking aspect of paths moving longitudinally is always associated with lateral zoning: every path laid through a space divides it. For this reason paths are always elements that articulate and define the space as well. The people on the path help to create the space themselves.

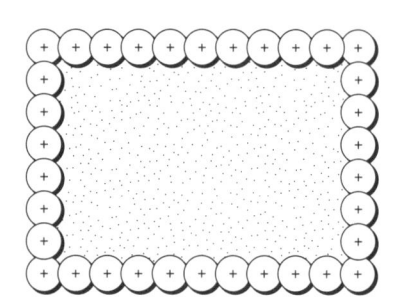

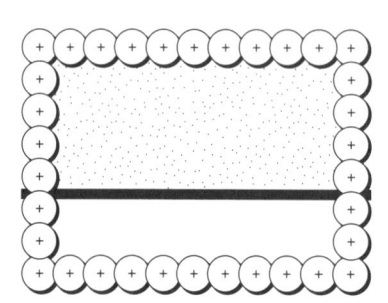

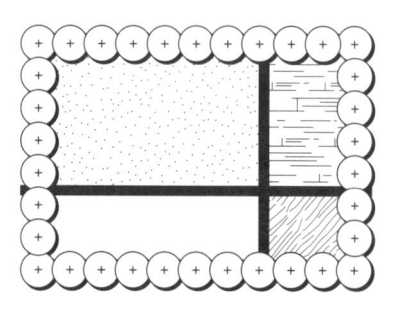

> A space

> Creating an area with a path

> Creating an area with paths

> People as boundaries

_**Creating scenes.** Paths create an effect not so much in their own right (surface etc.) but through the visual units, the scenes that open up as people move along. They direct the eye, draw attention to "sights". Paths present the space around them, they tell us "how to read" the qualities of their surroundings.

> *"What a lovely path," says Irene on her walk.*
> *Does she really mean the path?*

_**Pleasant progress.** The functional (landscape design) demands made on paths are lack of dependence on the weather (e.g. no puddles after rain) and ease of use (no unduly steep sections, or sections with frequently changing inclines, a surface that it is good to walk on etc.) [42].

[42] Cf. pp. 103-104: Proceeding "inattentively".

_**Considerate treatment of existing features.** Access focuses and controls movement. Thus the correct way through or avoidance of areas that are sensitive to being walked on (nature conservation units, long grass meadows etc.) is an important contribution to protecting existing features. Offering an attractive path structure that provides guidance helps to prevent people straying into sensitive areas.

> *Access always implies exclusion as well.*

— **Path and goal**

An access system is all the more successful the more interesting destinations are built in as a matter of course, and the more clearly users are supported in their instinctive urge to reach a (particular) goal. The less intrusive a (necessary) deviation from the line of the path is, the more "palatable" attractive reference points are made to the user, the less shifts in the line of the path will be seen as constraints on forward movement ("positive control"). Intermediate goals are particularly significant here: they give users a feeling of "having achieved something" at regular intervals, of "having arrived" or of being on the way towards something. This strengthens motivation to stay on the path.

In contrast with this, "negative control" makes people feel that they are being prevented from reaching their destination, and that they are having to tackle or avoid obstacles. This usually means that they leave the prescribed path to reach their chosen goal more directly. If this is not possible, they feel uncomfortable and annoyed.

_**Directly goal-oriented** paths' chief feature is that the chosen goal is visible and can be reached directly; it is the most natural way of organizing paths, and the one closest to the way people move forward naturally.

Starting-point │ ─ ─ ─ ─ ─ ─ ─ ─ ─ ─ ─ ─ ─ ─ ─ ─ ─ ─▶ destination

> *Directly goal-oriented*

▬Shifted goal-oriented paths shift slightly off the direct line of movement to the goal. Here it is advisable that the destination is not visible too soon, to minimize the temptation to walk through directly. Attractive intermediate goals (seating, viewing point, special plants etc.) are used to distract from the direct line to the destination (positive control).

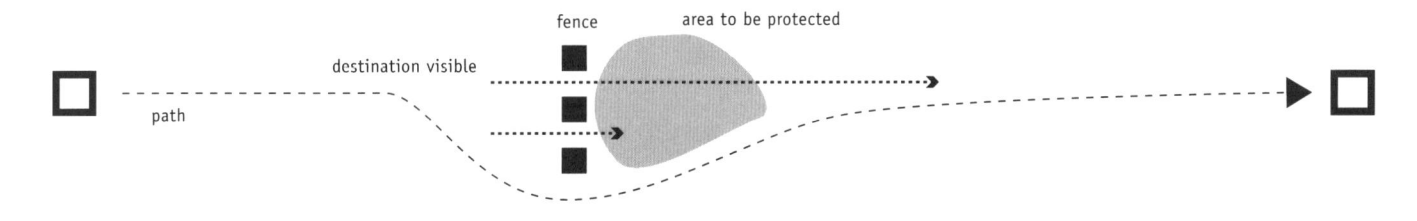

> *Negative control: goal-oriented, blocked – instinctive urge to take the direct route*

> *Positive control: diverted path – main destination not visible, motivation to divert comes from intermediate goal*

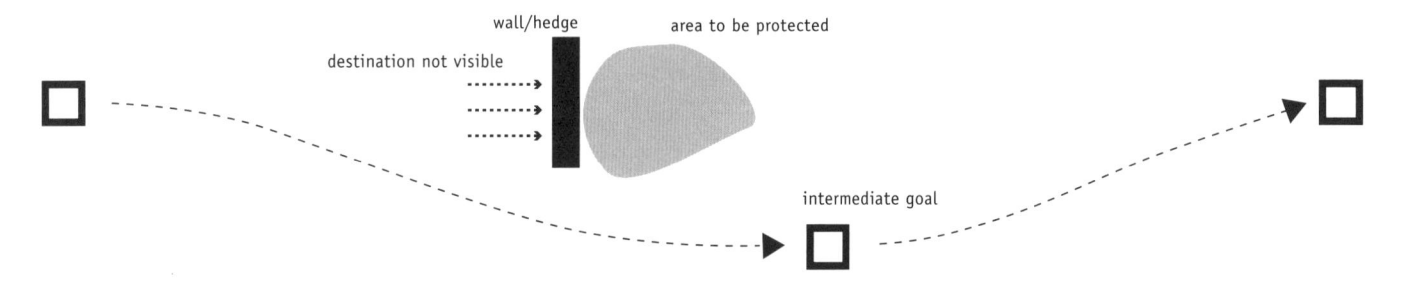

Rapid progress to a particular destination is not always the main aim. There are also freer links with targets where the path is not just a way of reaching the main destination but movement as such is important. ▬**Indirectly goal-oriented** movement types include hiking (long distances, close to nature), walking ("getting a breath of fresh air", no major effort involved), strolling and sauntering (in town, seeing and being seen, as easy as possible).

Indirectly goal-oriented movement also requires positive control. Every movement, even if it is almost entirely for its own sake, (e.g. jogging), involves attention to markers and special features (intermediate goals) along the route; these become – consciously or unconsciously – motives for continuing in the same direction or for moving off in a different direction. Intermediate destinations along a route are particularly important for indirectly goal-oriented movement in that they enhance the experience it offers and its quality with a wide range of features (possible stopping places, playgrounds, visual links etc.). The quality of a good access system depends to a large extent on the number of attractive intermediate destinations.

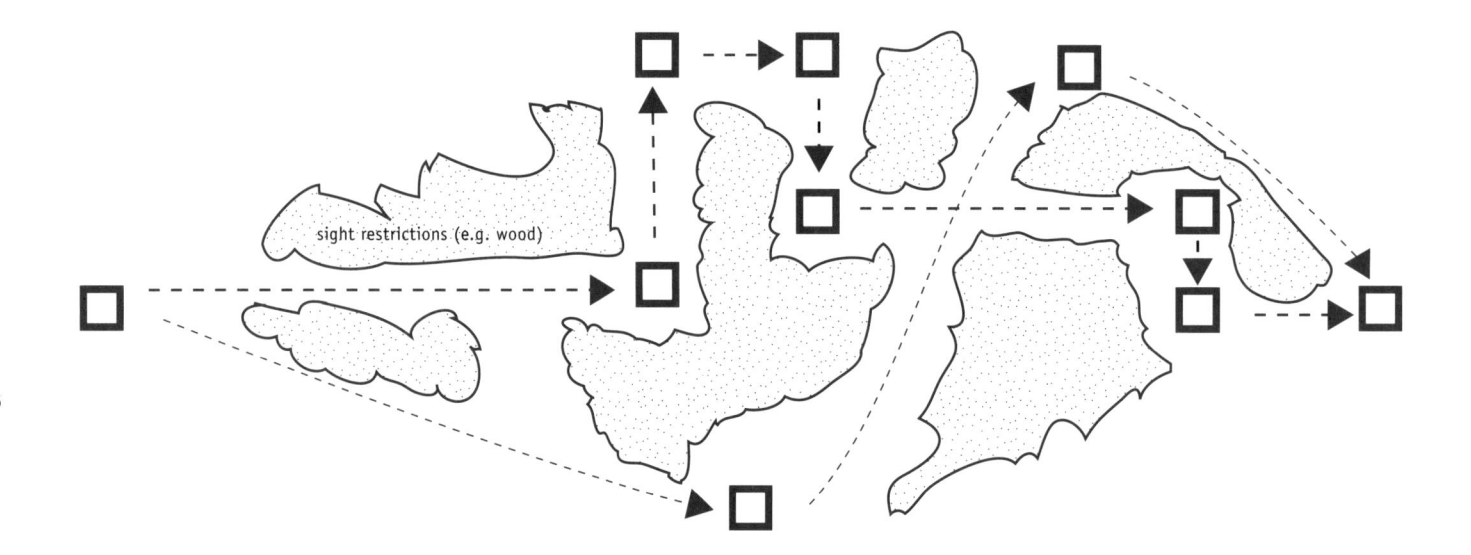

> *Indirectly goal-oriented (intermediate destinations become important, final destination has no priority)*

117

Path routing and visual links

Goal-oriented paths insist that the destination is reached rapidly. The line of the path expresses this by running straight on the level or by taking the least irksome route through rolling terrain. The whole path's perception field is primarily directed at the intended destination.

> "Automatic" field of perception from a straight path (sight corridor for precise perception: approx. 15°, mid-range perception field: 30-35°)

This does not apply to paths that are less goal-oriented. Shifting the line provides visual access to changing scenes/images. The path-line becomes a way of reading the open space. A wide range of images increases the attraction of the progress made (hiking, walking etc.) considerably.

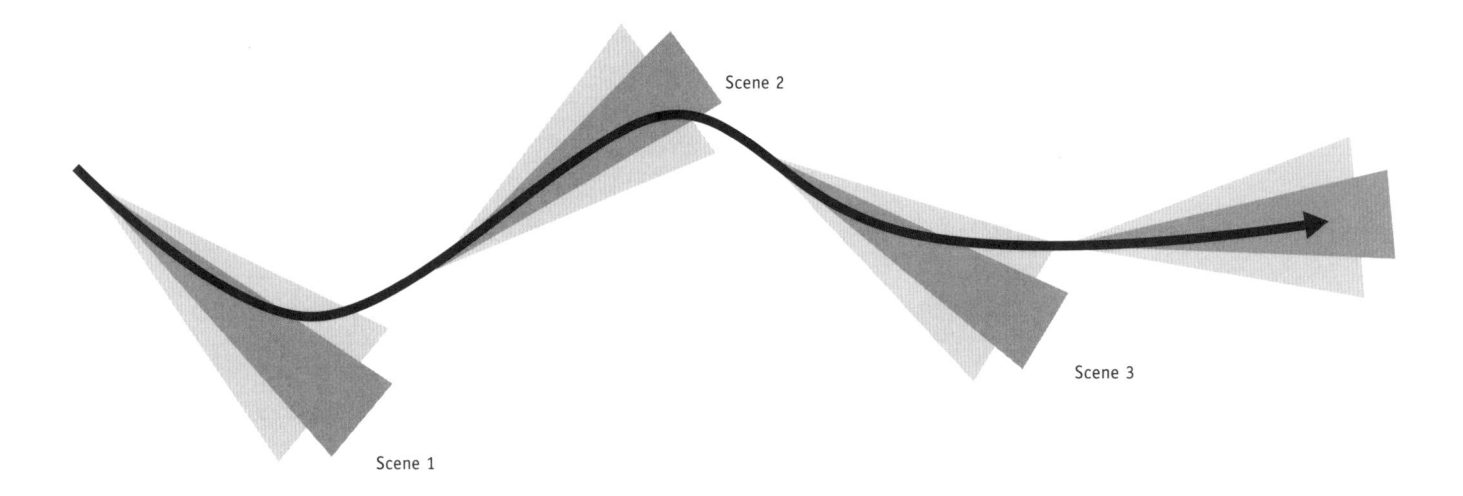

Scene 2

Scene 1

Scene 3

> Perception field for shifted routing – access to a wide range of scenes (but they have to be there to be seen!)

When setting up curved paths it is essential to avoid a (plan-) formal end in itself: every shift in the line of the path has to derive from actual topography (modelling) factors and/or scenic ones (attractive visual links). "Snaking" paths on flat terrain without directing, motivating aids (markers) seem arbitrary, irritating and tiring. They run counter to instinctive human movement and inevitably lead to site damage caused by people trampling short cuts.

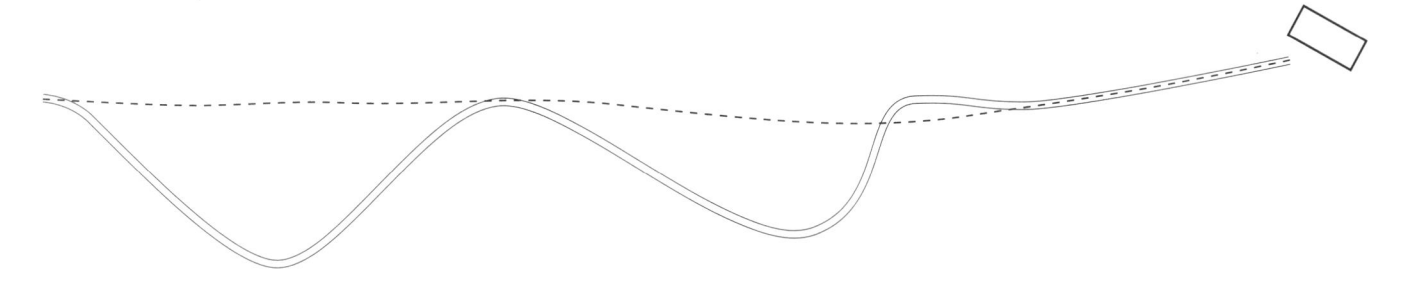

> *Curved path without scenic control. Consequence: paths trampled to shorten the route*

> *Curved path with open scenery (curves motivated by visual links and sight restrictions)*
[look for possible or necessary interventions for the way back]

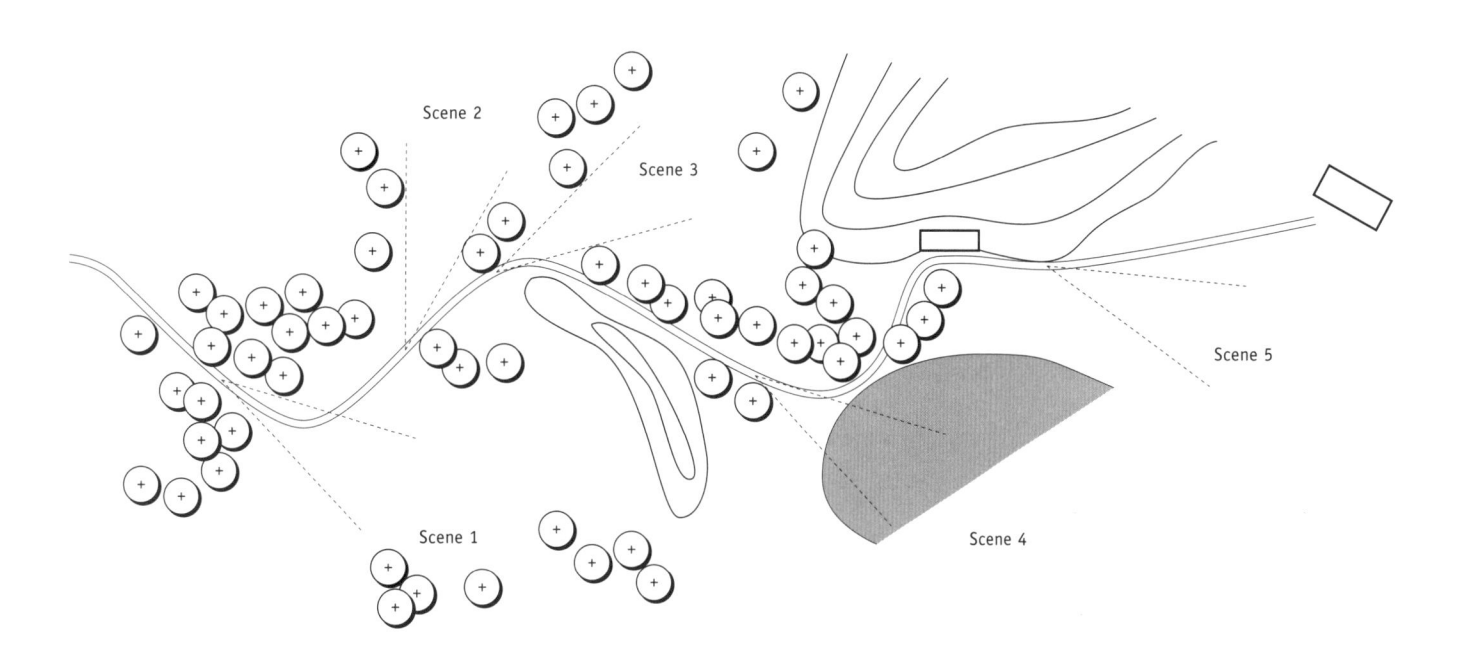

Path signs and markers

Paths are characterized as a rule by the fact that the path signs are the same **▪path surface** (material), **▪path width** and **▪path profile** (small-scale relief). This is how they convey coherence, reassure users that they are going the right way, so that they can relax

[43] Cf. p. 104-105: "Proceeding 'inattentively'".

and pay attention to their surroundings [43]. Changing certain characteristics of the path (e.g. changing the surface, changing the width etc.) draws attention back to the path, marks a change of significance (e.g. a junction), possibly means a change of orientation (Where am I? Where do I want to go?).

> *Path – coherence, security*

> *Changes of path characteristics – change of orientation*

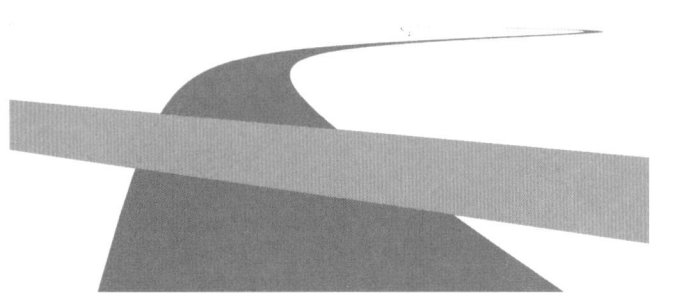

As well as the signs inherent in the path, the use of path markers [44] is another way to non-compulsory (positive) control. **▪Path**

[44] Cf. p. 103: "Anticipatory orientation".

markers are individual measures taken along the path in addition to a surface that is comfortable to walk on, encouraging people to stay on the path at certain places.

Making the path **▪**lower than its surroundings is one of the most natural and oldest path markers. Paths should definitely be slightly

[45] Cf. p. 109: "Beaten track – the archetypal path".

sunken in flat terrain in particular. Even sinking them by 5-15 cm means that users clearly feel less "need" to leave the route (the path), and vegetation accompanying the path reinforces the sense of direction by enhancing the small-scale relief.

Sinking the path by 30 to 50 cm creates a very strong controlling effect without making the user feel "isolated" from the surroundings. Further sinking does increase the sense of control, but particularly in the case of narrow paths and/or steep embankments creates a feeling of being constrained (up to approx. 100 cm) or of definitely being "shut in" (over 150 cm) [46]. Highly sunken paths only seem comfortable if accompanied by very shallow embankments and/or if the path is very wide.

[46] Cf. p. 80: "Height differences and spatial effect"

> Sunk by 5-15 cm

> Extra height given by vegetation

> Sunk by approx. 100 cm

As well as (small-scale) relief, individual features accompanying the path can give a strong sense of direction. A wide range of open-air elements are suitable for this (from tree to policeman). Path markers can accompany a path in the form of a line (e.g. hedges, banks, walls) or intermittently (benches, lamps, sculptures etc.).

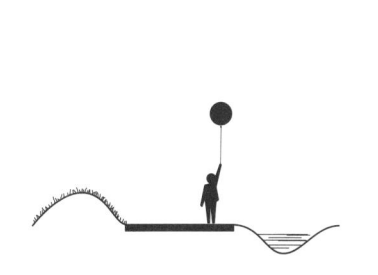

> Bank or ditch

> Grass or shrubs

> Bench or wall

> Lamp etc. etc.

Trees as path markers

Trees are probably the most frequently found single solid elements in landscape architecture. As rows they clearly reinforce the (path) direction, as single trees or groups of trees they identify important orientation points (intermediate goals). When using trees as path markers it is important to note that people's instinctive movement in relation to trees does not relate (in terms of ground plan) to the crown of the tree but (when close by), the control effect comes from the location of the trunk; people typically pass the trunk at a distance of 70-150 cm.

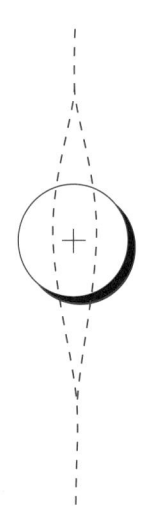

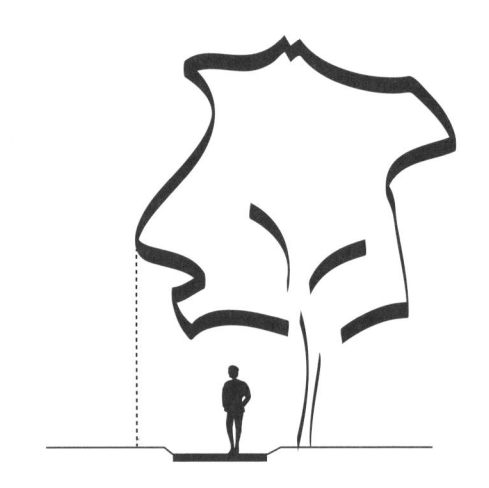

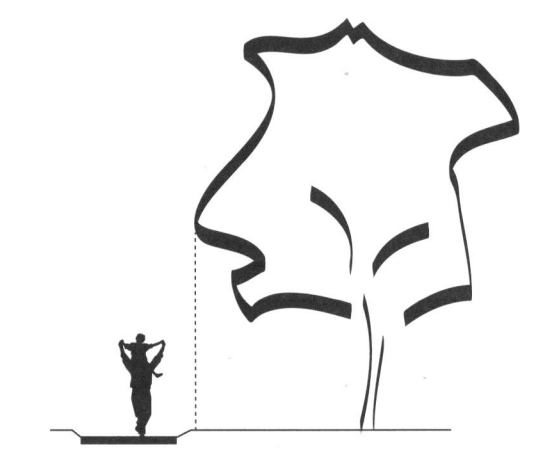

> *Typical line for walking around a tree*

> *Correct: the route of the path relates to the trunk (about 70-150 cm away)*

> *Incorrect: the route of the path relates to the crown. (Typical mistake made on a plan!) A path will probably be trampled close to the trunk alongside the intended route*

Avenues are rows of trees, preferably of uniform species and habit, planted at equal intervals along a straight (or slightly curved) line. They are one of the most powerful ways of directing movement available to landscape architecture.

> Single-row avenue

> Double-row avenue ("genuine" avenue)

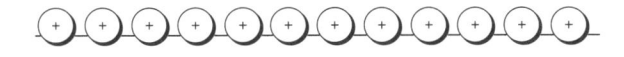

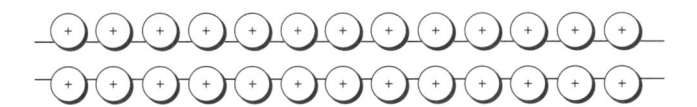

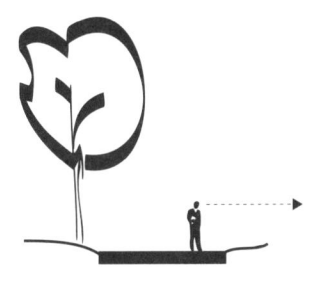

▪ Single-row avenues are path markers that clearly relate to the surrounding area, whereas ▪ avenues with two rows of trees tend to be strongly self-referential, and create space in their own right. Two-row avenues make the same effect as a regular sequence of gateways: here adjacent individual trees should ideally be placed in the normal way in relation to the line of the path. This creates a strong sense of path movement direction, and also produces possible side openings ("avenue windows").

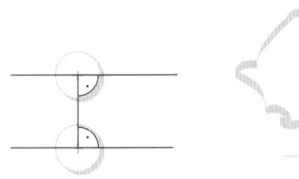

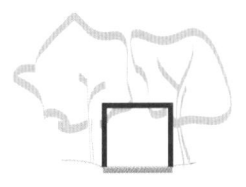

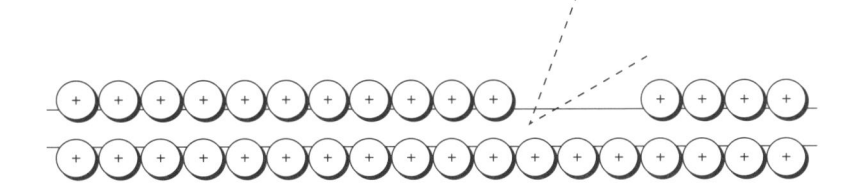

> Avenue – sequence of gates

> Avenue window

> **Colonnades and arcades**

Two-row avenues can create space in the form of colonnades or arcades. Typical ▬tree colonnades are made up of tree species with a column-like or narrow pyramid profile planted relatively far apart. Colonnades evoke an almost solemn mood, and tend towards being "more public" in character.

Trees that grow to a considerable width create spaces that are closed to the sky, ▬tree arcades. Their mood is calm, protective, "private". Further differentiation in the possible moods induced by arcades (between light and darkness, light-green or dark-green shadows, patches of light or dark green areas etc.) is achieved by chosing the appropriate species.

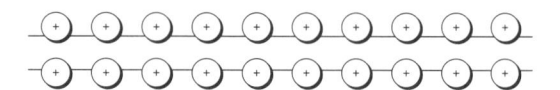

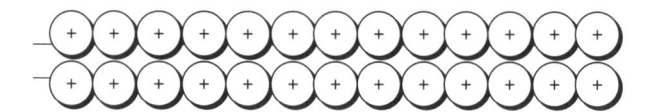

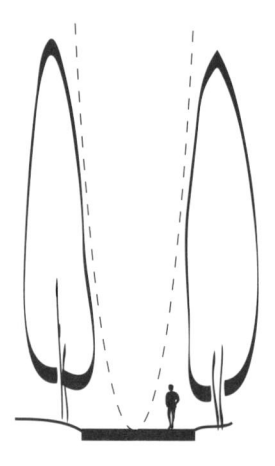

> Tree colonnade

> Tree arcade

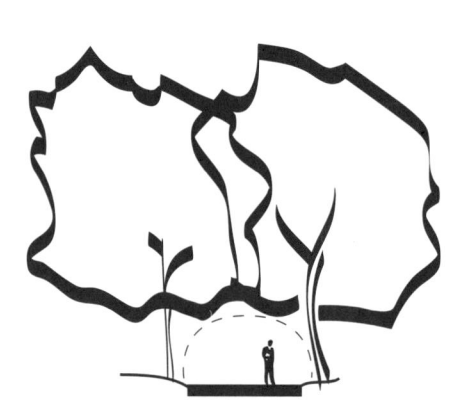

125

Path joints

Path joints are special, small-scale situations "on the way"; they mean change. Path joints are ▬ways through and entrances (crossing spatial boundaries), ▬steps and ramps (dealing with changes in height), ▬junctions (where routes or paths meet) and ▬way-stations (stopping points or points of repose). They are very suitable as locations for shifting the route of a path.

▬Through ways, entrances. Paths should meet boundaries at right angles [47]. Accompanying measures can be taken to prepare

[47] Cf. p. 96: "The straight line and the right angle".

paths that lead obliquely to boundaries for the necessary shift. These include swinging the path to be at right angles to the boundary at an early stage, creating areas immediately before the boundary that are neutral in their direction or making the boundary respond to the direction the path is taking.

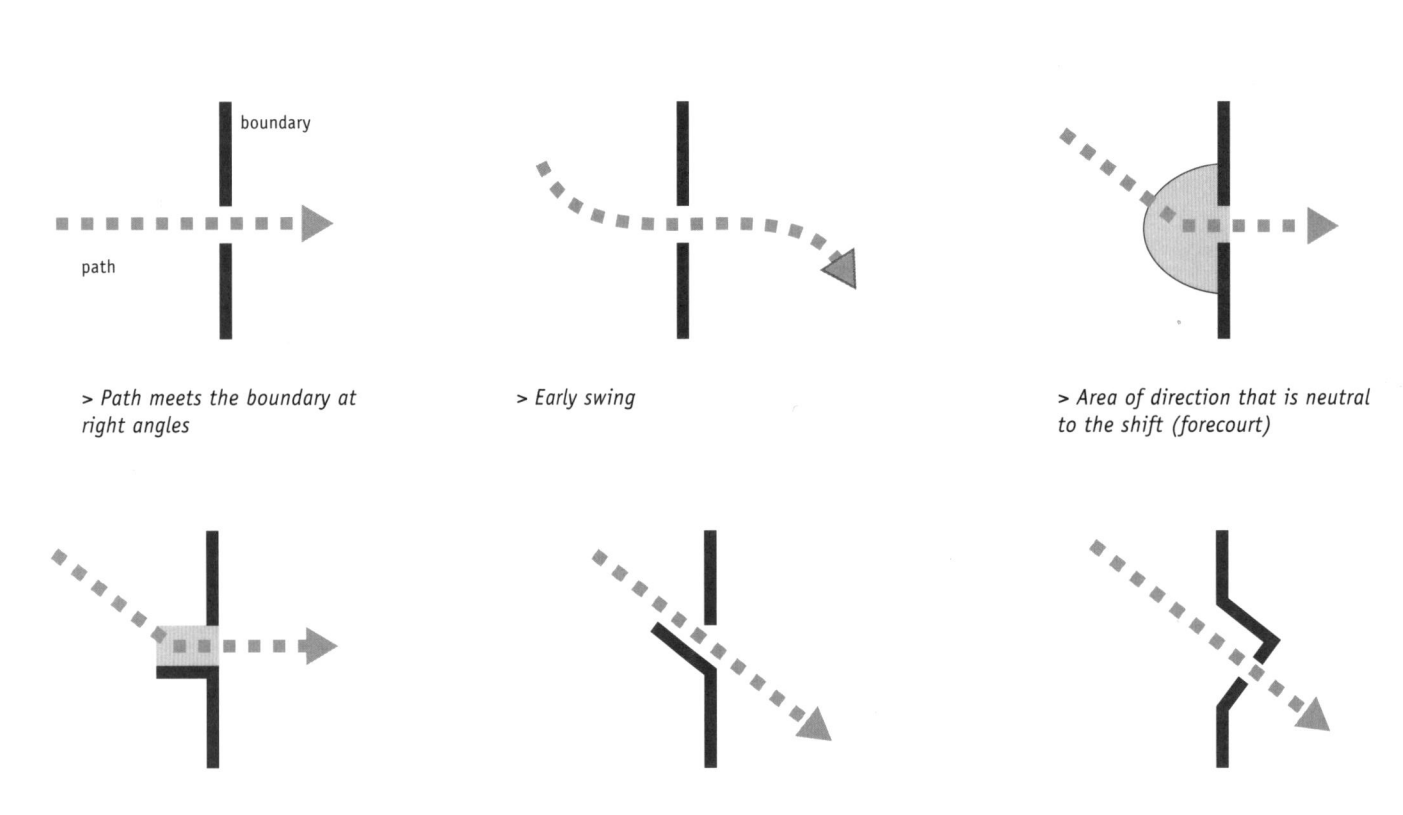

> Path meets the boundary at right angles

> Early swing

> Area of direction that is neutral to the shift (forecourt)

> Addition to the boundary (same material!). Good solution in combination with a little forecourt

> Swung addition to the boundary

> Shifting the boundary in the area where the path goes through (path vertical to the boundary)

_Steps always indicate direction powerfully. The areas immediately in front should be specially characterized to prepare for the change of direction. Therefore steps, relative to stringers or the edges of a building, should either be pulled forward (inviting, public) or set back (more restricting, more private). Combining steps that have been brought forward with offset stringers is an effective means of motivating direction swings and identifying principal directions ("positive control").

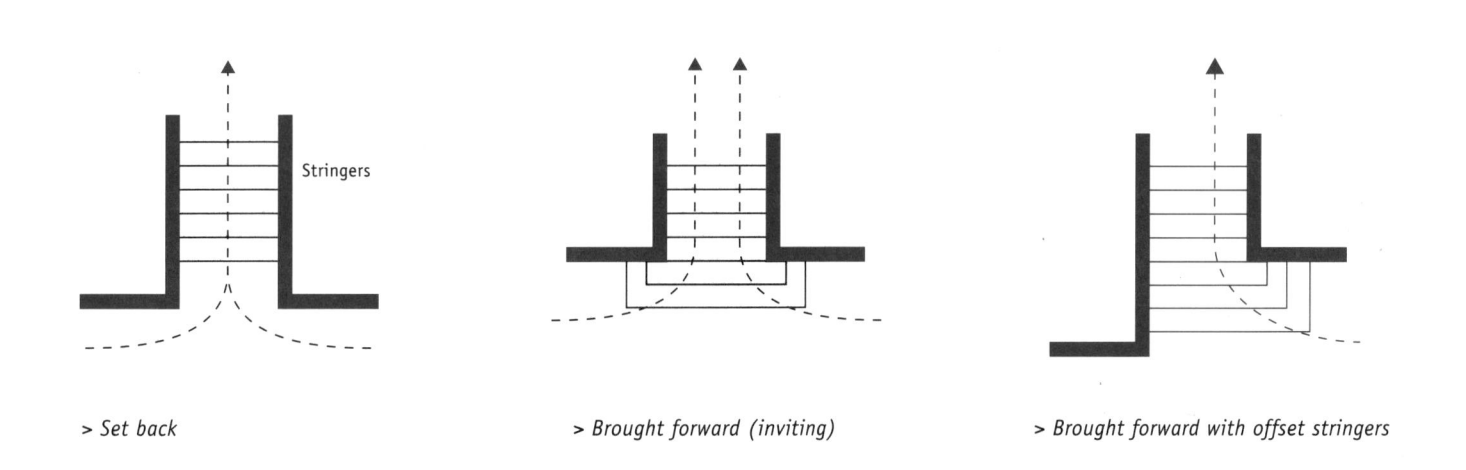

> Set back

> Brought forward (inviting)

> Brought forward with offset stringers

_Path junctions are "joints" that (unlike road junctions) require areas of repose. Here users stop moving and can withdraw from the stream of movement to watch it, to rest and to get their bearings where necessary. To guarantee this, the "joint" should be wider, and offer a greater area than the cross sections of the paths that are meeting. But widening alone does not automatically produce an inviting joint in the path.

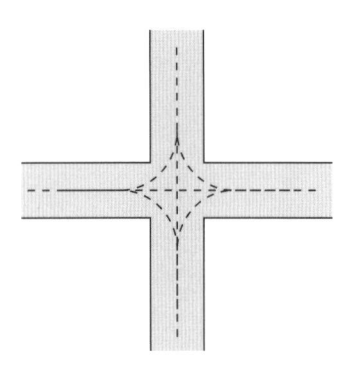

> *The classic road junction has no points of repose*

> *This enlargement does not make a good joint for the paths: capped corners are not areas of repose, but the area with the most traffic in them*

> *Rounding off is no better, it just creates an absence of corners*

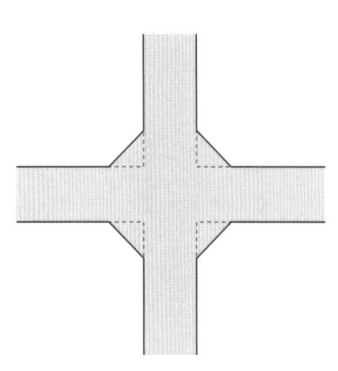

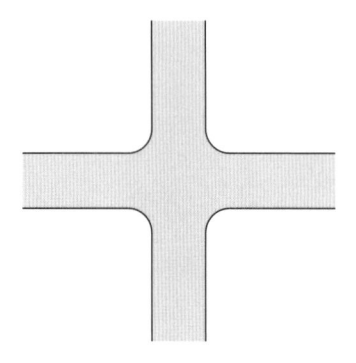

So the aim is to create areas for stopping in, and to keep these areas off the main movement line. This can be achieved by offsetting, for example; this avoids creating "infinitely long" views of the path and creates "stopping places", intermediate goals.

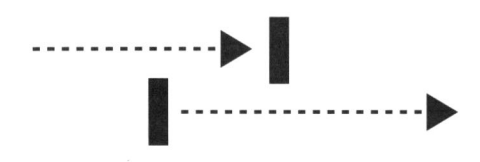

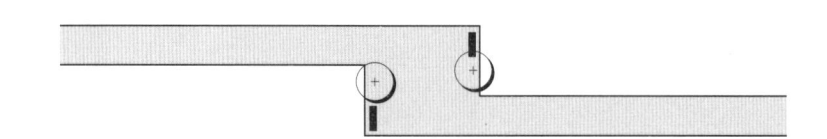

> *Offsetting*

> *Offset point as a stopping-place (with the basic building bricks of repose, "bench and tree")*

> Radially offset intersecting paths (so-called "turbine"), benches in the quiet zones (note links to views and protected backs!)

> Extending the joint, benches with trees on each side (dashes: main movement lines)

> Expanding the joint, calming with bench "havens"

> Expanding the joint, unmistakable place for sitting

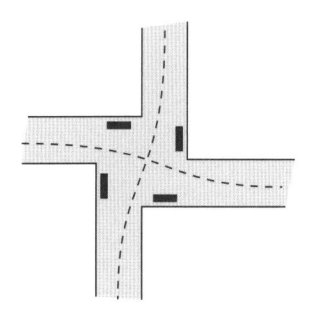

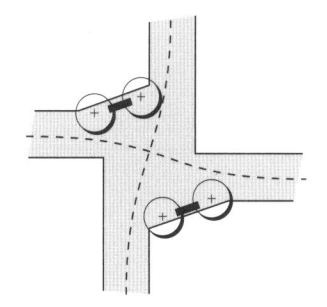

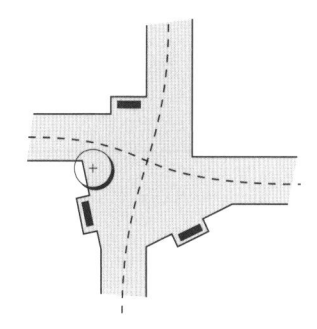

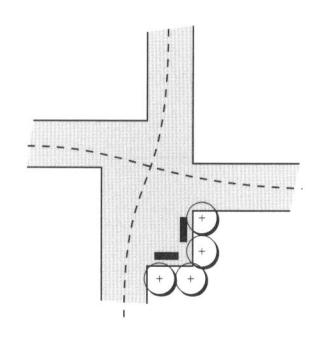

Path joints are, with differentiation using different widths for the path, a way of imposing an access line hierarchy [48]. Equal status path intersections bring together (and distribute) paths of similar status, different widths make certain combinations of paths more inviting, "more important" (e.g. main direction for the path) and down-grade others by means of shape, indicating the lesser importance of the available destinations.

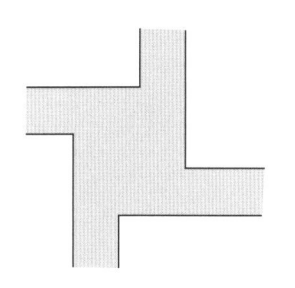

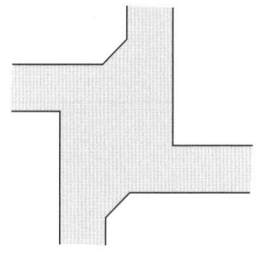

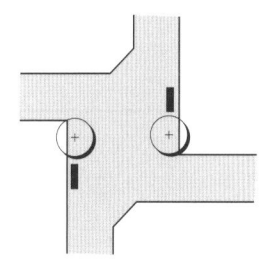

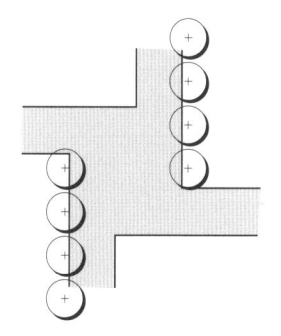

[48] Cf. also p. 134: "Path networks".

> Equal status junction – all directions have the same value

> Hierarchical junction – "opening" the corners makes the north-south link "more important"

> Additional marking of the end (beginning) of the side paths (bench, tree)

> Single-row avenues make the path hierarchy clearer

> *Hierarchical junctions – different path widths [Look at the differences between the variants for yourself.]*

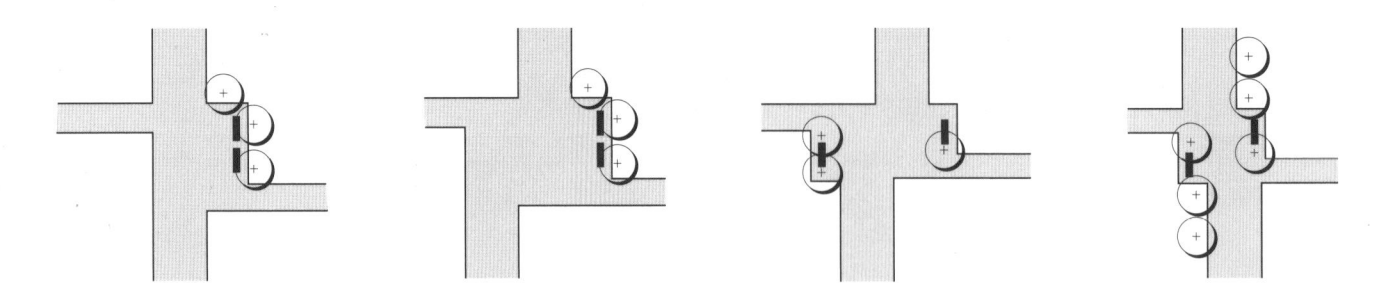

If lines of movement meet linear structures (paths, edges of the space etc.) outside the (directionally neutral) right angle, this leads to "automatic" direction to the "open" angle (greater than 90°) [49].

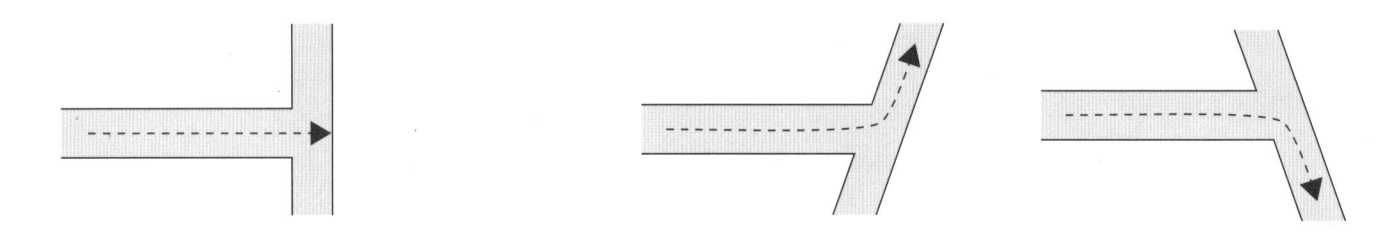

[49] Cf. p. 96 "The straight line and the right angle"

> *Junction at right angles – directionally neutral*

> *Line of movement meets the path at an acute angle – directs to the "open" angle*

> *Tripartite junctions. [Take a close look: Direction? Areas of repose? Lines of movement? Path hierarchy? Where would you put the classic bench and/or tree if appropriate? What would be the consequences for the areas formed at the point where the paths join?]*

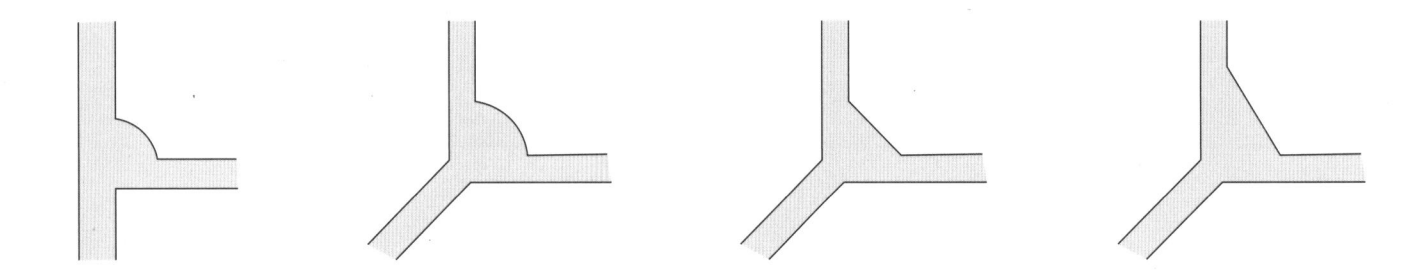

**Stopping places** are broader areas along a path. They break up long runs of pathway [50], provide resting places on the way, but without giving a sense of being excluded from the flow of the path, from everything that is new, different, coming past. Stopping places should not be "by" the path, but visibly form part of it. If isolation is required (e.g. protected children's playgrounds) these areas should not be niches by the path, but clearly secluded, with a little path of their own for access.

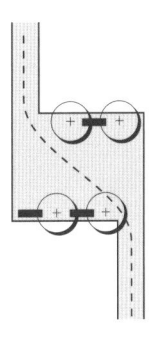

[50] Cf.p.129: "Turbine". Offset on long runs of path.

<1> Stopping-place as a joint in the path – interrupting a long run of pathway

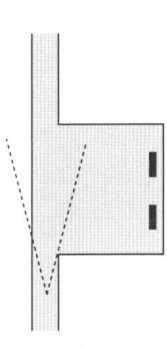

<2> Niche "by" the path – neither part of the path nor really separate. Mainly out of the field of vision (30-35°), long view retained. Not to be recommended

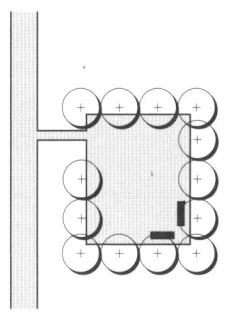

<3> Better: independent unit – clearly apart from the path, access by its own path. Change of use (e.g. children's playground)

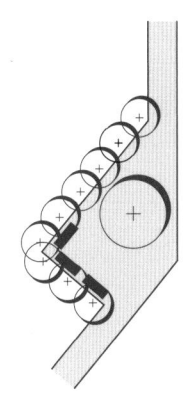

<4> and <5> Stopping-place where the path swings – maintaining a link with the direction of the paths by being at right angles to the main movement line, stopping place is part of the path. Better than example <2>

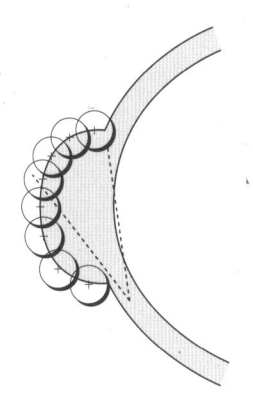

<6> Stopping place at the apex of a curve in the path – clearly "in the field of vision". Functionally similar to <4> and <5>

> *The seat (or bench) – a (stopping) behaviour archetype*

Benches are essential "building bricks" for open space, complementing movement and offering a clear invitation to stop and rest. A bench is "right" only with regard to its surroundings. There are three crucial criteria here: ▪quiet(er) surroundings ("bench area"), ▪something special to look at (e. g. clear view of a busy urban square, facing a striking landscape, the approaching path etc.) ▪protected back (by a wall, hedge, tall grass, tree-trunk, terrace etc.).

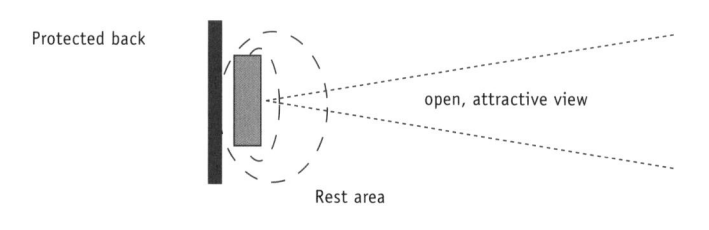

Benches placed along the way should not be "in the way" (exception: very wide paths where the benches can "create" their own quiet area). Otherwise little alcoves (bench "havens") by the path are better. Here the bench should have a little space in front of it: 30-60 cm (no more!)> Protection at the side from trees is also to be recommended (though this variant also needs wider paths), Benches placed at right angles to each other in stopping-places create situations that are much more likely to produce communication.

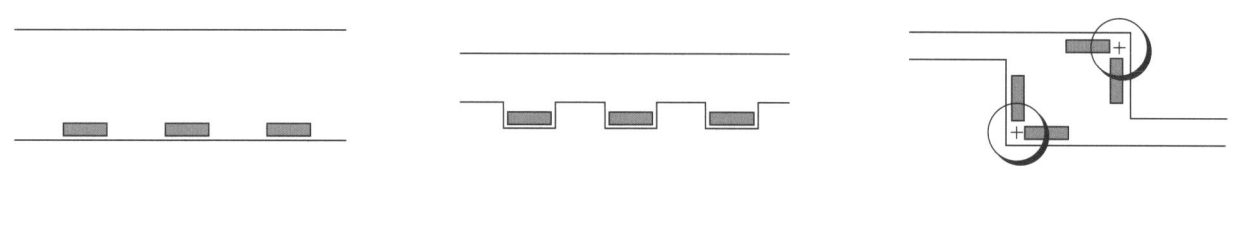

> *Bench on the path – possible for very wide paths*

> *Bench havens*

> *Usually better: stopping-place with benches (additionally marked with trees)*

133

▬ Network of paths

There are three basic internal access types: the ▬**hierarchical** network of paths offers routes with graduated significance (and usefulness). Starting with the principal paths (promenades, axes etc.) – usually determined by external goals - less important and less used paths (side paths) are offered, and possibly also delicate ramifications of additional trails (tracks). The main paths are usually distinguished from less important ones by wider average cross sections, more durable surfaces (often for both pedestrians and cyclists) and special materials or furniture. A hierarchical network makes sense if a number of functions and needs have to be met (and accessed) within an open-air complex. An ▬**equal status** network helps if all the criteria affecting it (external destinations, use requirements etc.) are of roughly similar importance. An ▬**incomplete** hierarchy handles the flow of movement efficiently on the one hand (principal paths) and then juxtaposes them with a complementary network of fine veins (tracks) for (secluded, lonely) exploration of the area.

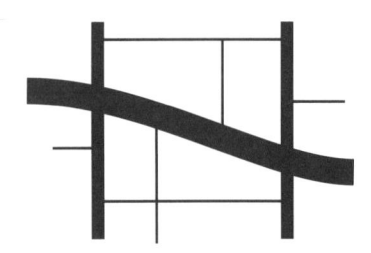

> Hierarchical path network –
main path, side path, track

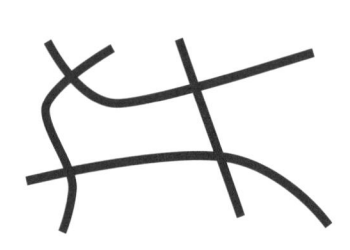

> Equal status path network

> Incomplete hierarchy –
main path, track

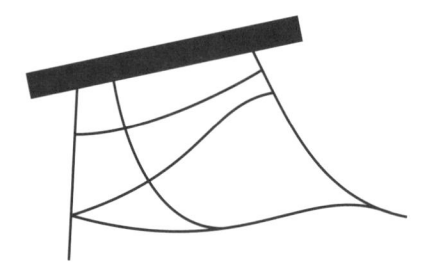

▬ Path routing and use of the area

High quality access is (also) judged by its potential for creating or retaining useful spaces for people to experience. This is why paths are often laid along boundaries: the mutual disturbance caused by linear movement (path) and use of the area (e.g. play or rest areas) can be minimized by this, and larger areas remain coherent units. The boundary is also additionally strengthened by the path running by it.

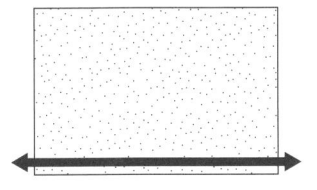

> Access, along the edge – an area that is to be used

> Access, axially off-centre – two areas with different potential uses (e.g. spacious play area next to quiet area)

> Access along the central axis – two areas of equal status (only makes sense for very large spaces)

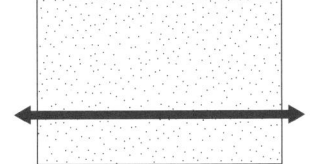

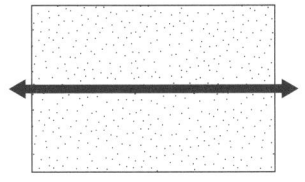

Smaller areas "tolerate" diagonal paths (relative to the boundary) badly, as they create "corners" that are of only limited use and represent an undue formal imposition on spaces [51]. From a gardening perspective, pointed, cramped corners are difficult to maintain (mowing etc.), i.e. they rapidly become unprepossessing. If diagonal paths cannot be avoided (e.g. because destinations or boundaries cannot be shifted), the greatest possible attempt should at least be made to swing the paths so that they meet the boundary at right angles [52].

[51] Cf. also p. 97 ff.: "Emphasized focal points".
[52] Cf. also p. 126: "Path joints", ways through, entrances.

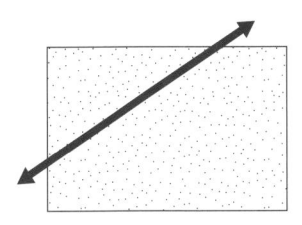

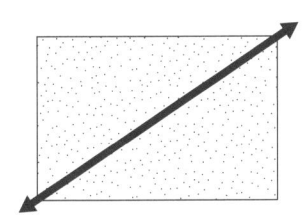

> Access diagonal to existing boundaries – little opportunity to use the (left-over) areas

> Diagonal access – swung to approach the boundary at right angles

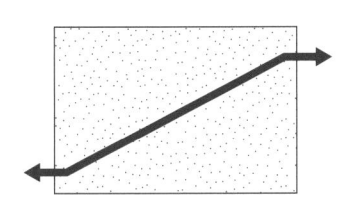

Path routing and spatial shapes

The circle is the only shape that is entirely neutral in terms of direction. All other (spatial) shapes indicate a particular direction more

[53] Cf. also p. 94: "Special position". | or less strongly: this can establish reference points and reinforce the path routing considerably [53].

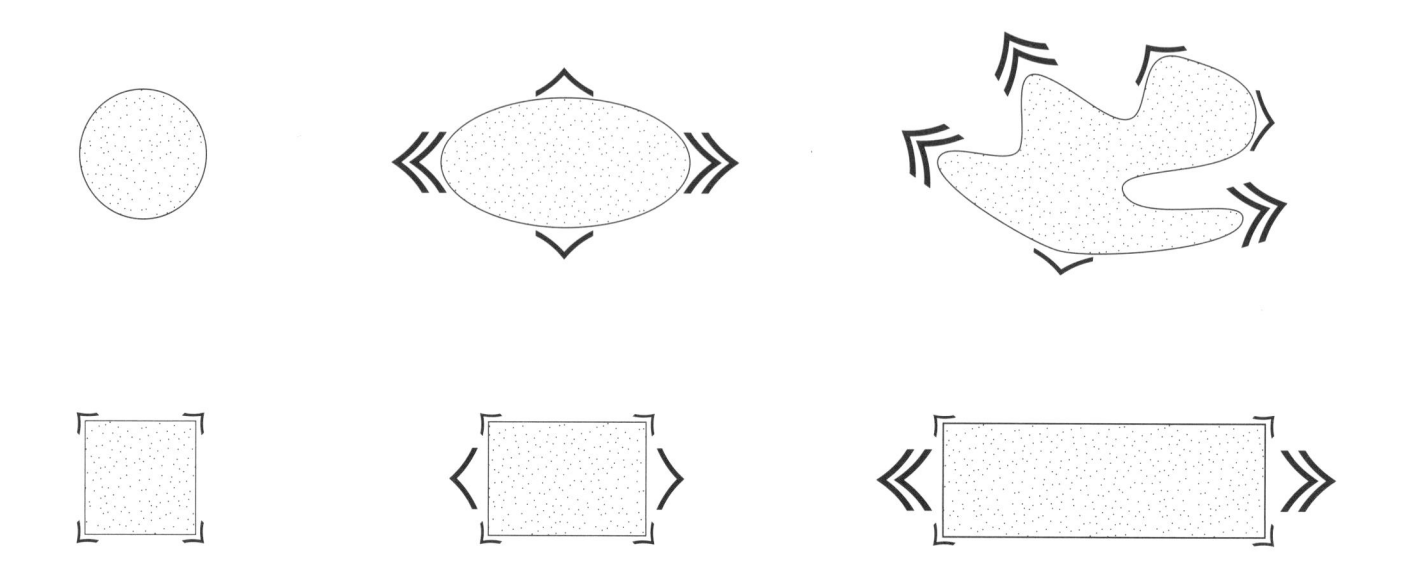

> Direction indicated with varying degrees of strength by different (spatial) shapes

Access lines that follow a strongly dominant direction within spaces or parts of spaces "automatically" offer guidance ("positive control"): the directional nature of the path and of the space are mutually reinforcing. Paths that are clearly routed against the dominant direction within a space do not provide this guidance. Spaces that tend to become unduly long can even be minimized in their directional effect when strong paths "cross" them.

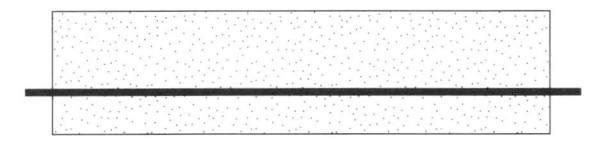

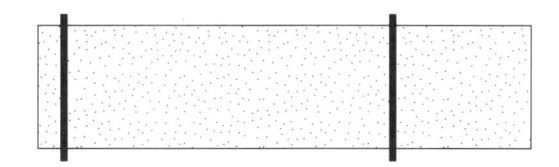

> *Spatial direction dominance and path give each other mutual support – the space is made "even longer" by the route chosen for the path*

> *Paths at right angles to the dominant direction "shorten" the space*

> *Directional shape*

> *Strengthening the strongest indication of direction – path running along the dominant line within the dominant direction of the space*

> *Weakening the dominant directional effect by crossing (path meets the dominant line at right angles)*

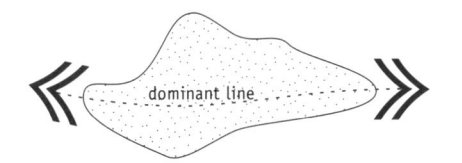

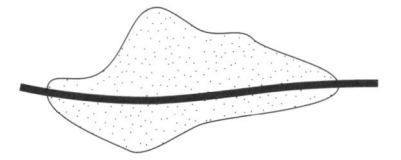

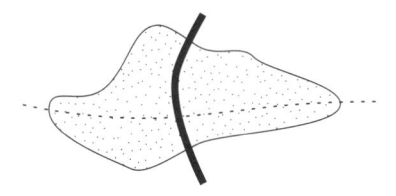

137

Less directional spaces provide only weak reference points for routing paths, the path itself has to "direct". Reference points for path routing in less directional, level, large spaces are: routing along individual partial direction indications in the space (dominant lines); routing parallel with nearby or dominant boundaries; routing using the geometrical focal point of a space unit; routing using the most distant – or, alternatively, the obviously closest –, point of the boundary in terms of general direction.

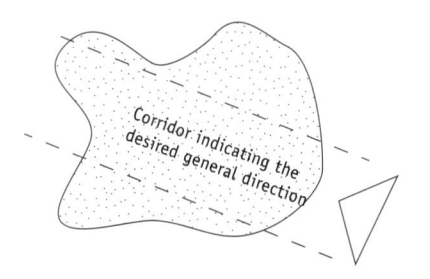

> Space with free boundaries, level, no dominant direction

> Dominant lines in the areas within the directional corridor

> Important reference points

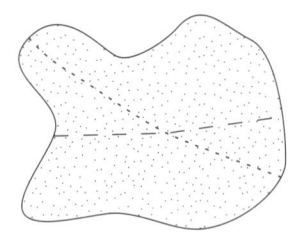

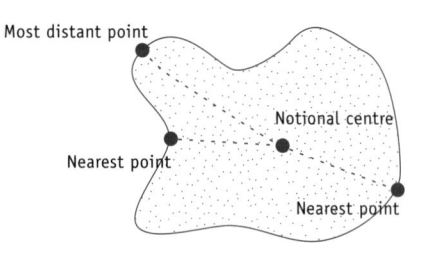

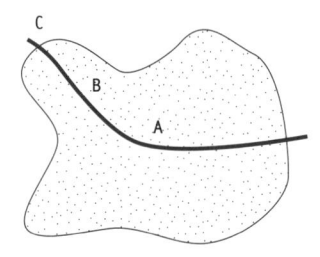

<1> Good line for the path (in very large spaces) through notional centre A, notional dominant line B and most distant point C

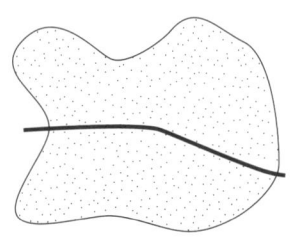

<2> Less strong line than <1>, nevertheless a more useful way of creating discrete areas in smaller spaces

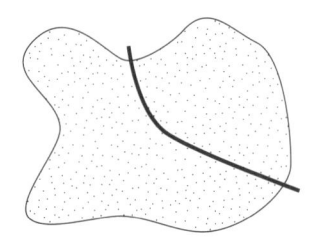

<3> Look for yourself. Discrete areas formed? Dominant lines? In large or small spaces?

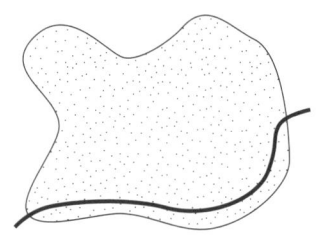

<4> Generous, unified area and strong sense of direction by taking the path along the boundary; the only way of opening up possibilities for use independent of the path in small spaces (unfortunately outside our corridor)

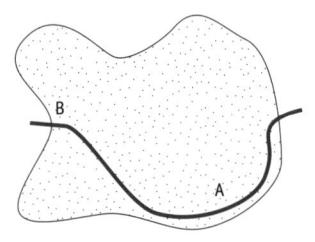

<5> Path running parallel to boundary A to the closest point in the general direction B – good use of positive guidance, good area-units, especially for smaller spaces

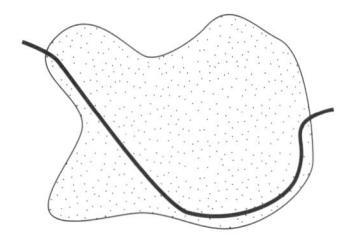

<5> Look for yourself

It is not only the shape of the boundary that imposes direction, but the main slope on the terrain as well. As a rule, directions running counter to the shape of the space or the shape of the terrain are to be avoided. This can be achieved by ▬ adapting the shape of the space to the shape of the terrain, in other words by placing new boundaries parallel with the (unchanged) directional dominance of the terrain, ▬ adapting the shape of the terrain to the spatial constraints, in other words changing the ground modelling while keeping the boundaries the same. If neither alternative is available (cost, property boundaries etc.), the response can be ▬ planting and creating sub-spaces directed according to the run of the terrain.

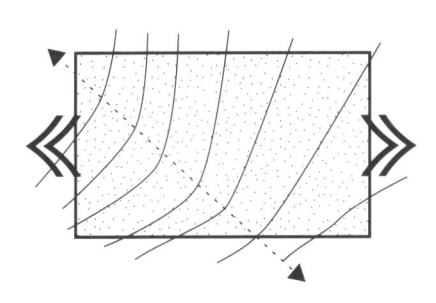

> *Present state of affairs: boundaries and terrain directed differently*

> *Changing the boundaries – boundaries respond to the direction of the terrain – the two direction coincide and reinforce each other*

> *Changing the modelling of the terrain – terrain modelling responds to the direction indicated by the boundaries*

> *No change to the boundaries or small-scale relief – directional sub-spaces adopt the direction indicated by the shape of the terrain (which naturally changes the range of uses the project can offer, as relatively small units are produced)*

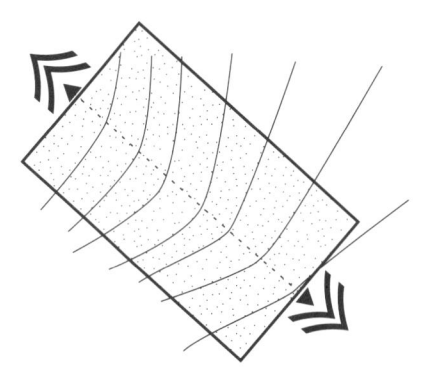

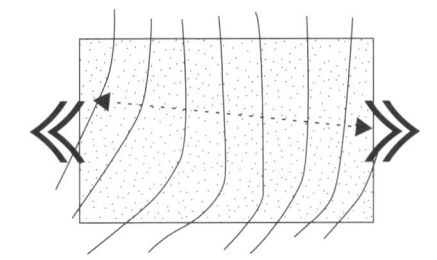

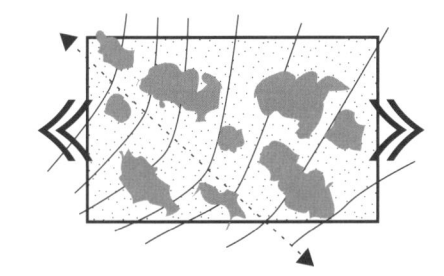

▬ Paths and spatial sequences

Paths are instructions about how to read spaces and (visual) links. The access mode affects the character of the space directly: ▬ **Direct access** (direct connection of a space to a route that has higher status) creates more public, less "peaceful" spaces with high communication levels, ▬ **indirect access** (path off the main route) produces calmer units with a greater degree of privacy.

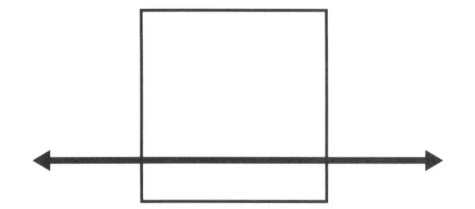

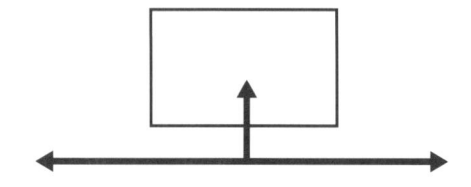

> Direct access; space more public, high degree of communication

> Indirect access – space calmer, more private

Spaces can be placed in a row along an access route or be grouped around it: ▬ **spatial sequences in rows** are a powerful aid to getting one's bearings, and so are suitable if the space or sequence of spaces has new users all the time (e.g. horticultural shows, tourist sites etc.). Axial connection, a particular form of the sequence based on rows, has a clear beginning and end, linking it together by different, often unconnected areas that are passed through. Axial links "lend" their starting or end points particular significance [54]. If this significance is not established or not feasible, axial connection becomes a questionable design resource.

[54] Cf. p. 91: "Focal points", start / end of directions.

> Straight spatial sequence in rows, with some direct, some indirect access

> Axial connection

Row-sequenced spaces have a high orientation value but have the disadvantage of relatively long distances to be covered to reach the individual spaces. _**Grouped spatial sequences** on the other hand offer excellent access (effective access, short distances to cover) but are harder for people to find their way around (the path alone is not sufficient as an orientation aid). _Spaces sequenced in linear groups create a juxtaposition of spaces with direct or indirect access with differing degrees of public quality. If spatial sequences are _interconnected, several spaces mesh together [55].

[55] Cf. p. 62: "Spatial sequences – spatial gradations".

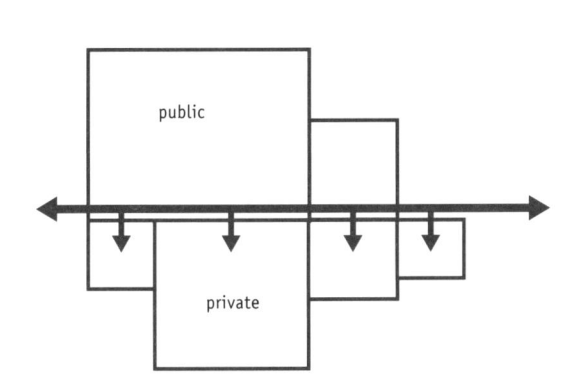

> Linear spatial sequence

> Spatial sequence as an interconnected group

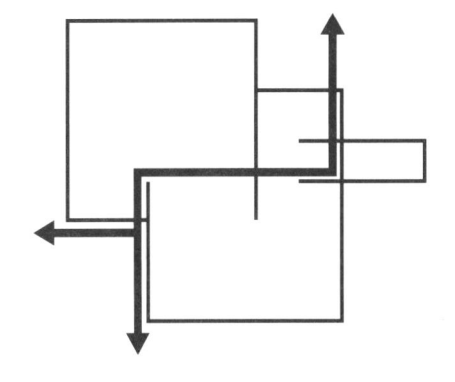

notes

ideas

quotations

sketches

questions

additions

[4] Design qualities

4.1 Fundamentals of good design

4.2 Characteristics of good design

4.3 Repetition as a tool

4.1 Fundamentals of good design

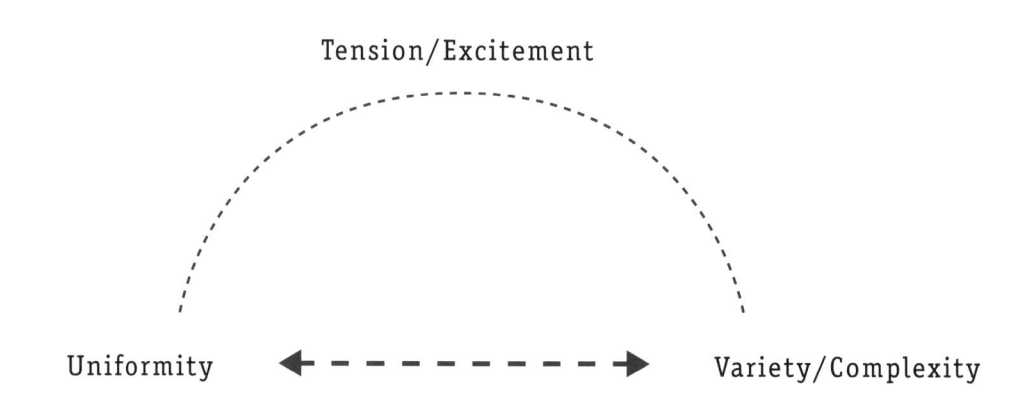

```
                    Tension/Excitement
                  . - - - - - - - .
                .′                 ′.
              .′                     ′.
             .                         .
            .                           .
         Uniformity  ←- - - - - - -→  Variety/Complexity
```

Design means coherence, and so requires that the component parts that create form should have things in common. By them, unity is achieved. But good design is more than that: it needs its share of variety, diversity, different components. This creates tension and excitement.

▬ Form and coherence

Design (in landscape architecture) involves ordering and arranging things to satisfy people's constant search for coherence, for connections. Coherence can be imposed on phenomena that are perceived as separate if we can bring them together as units on the basis of **common features** (similarities).

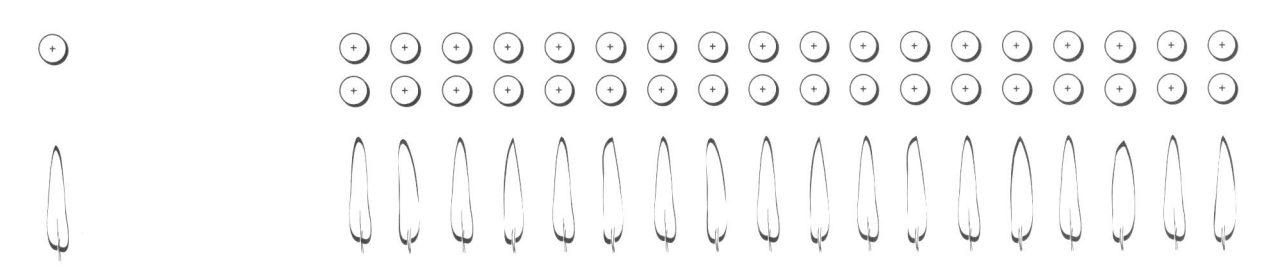

> Tree, columnar (like a cypress)

> Avenue, colonnade, but also Italy, Tuscany, Chianti …

We human beings are constantly trying to form links, to compare every new impression with our previous experience immediately and to test it for connections with its surroundings [56]. This process is in operation in our every (waking) moment. Its purpose is to classify phenomena that suddenly crop up as quickly as possible, to "occupy" our limited human "RAM" for as short a time as possible [57], to release it immediately to deal with new impressions and sort them out mentally; it is one of our most useful survival strategies.

[56] Cf. p. 91 "Creating focal points".
[57] Cf. p. 18: Superization as an aid to handling our limited ability to absorb impressions into our consciousness.

▬ Uniformity through common features

Creating coherence requires us to be able to relate different phenomena to each other on the basis of (at least) one similarity [58]. And so seeing or thinking about [59] coherence, about uniformity demands similar characteristics, (perceptibly) common features from things. We create uniformity on the basis of ▬**shared position** (proximity, arrangement, symmetry), of ▬**shared appearance** (shape or material) or of ▬**theoretical/thematic shared features.**

[58] The concept of "similarity" also includes "equality" as its (unattainable) extreme.
[59] Cf. p. 21: "Induction".

▬ Shared position

Positional relationships arise from the way individual things are placed relative to each other in a characteristic position that is ex-

[60] Cf. p. 91: "Creating focal points". | traordinary in the context. The "strength" of the connection created by position depends directly on the degree of this extraordinariness [60].

> *Positional relationship (e.g. closeness) . . . .*

> *. . . is a relative phenomenon*

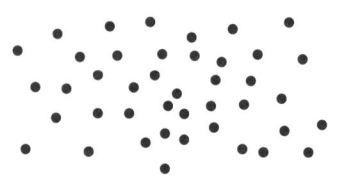

▬ **Closeness** as a positional relationship makes its effect by a relatively "small" distance between things. The closer the things are to each other (relative to the distance between other things in the context), the more strongly we perceive them as belonging together, as a unit.

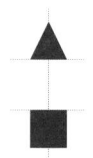

> *Closeness as a positional relationship*

_Arrangement makes its positional effect if things produce a common form familiar to the viewer on the basis of their particular position (e.g. line, circle, grid, symbol etc [61].) The simpler and more regular the arrangement is, the stronger will be the sense of uniformity, of connection between the things.

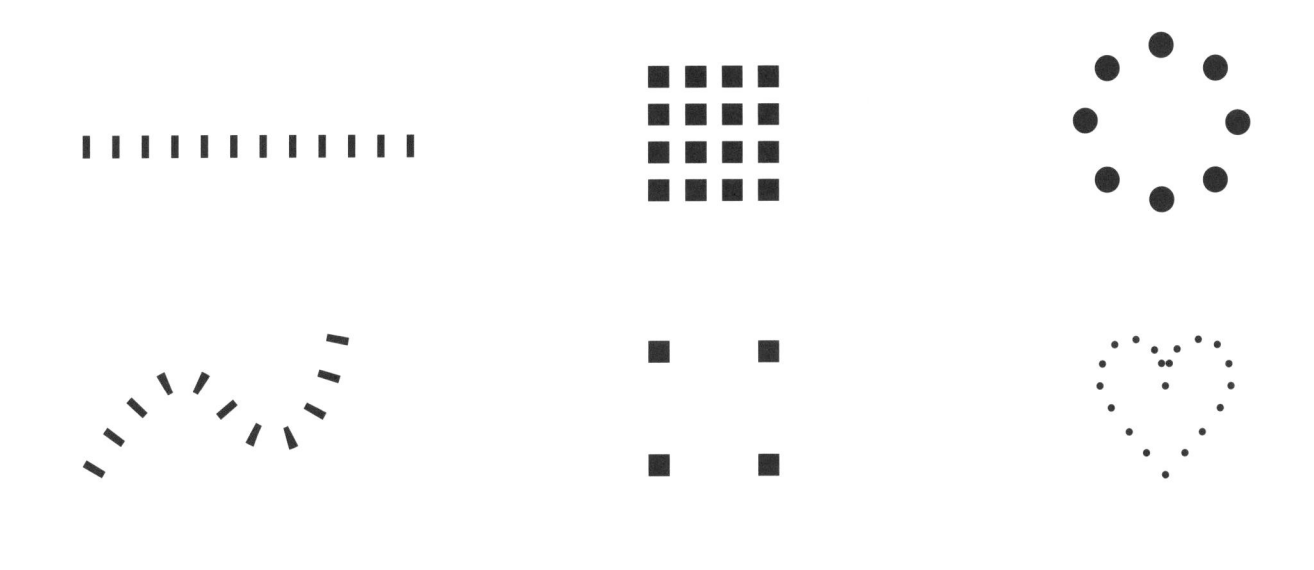

[61] Prior experience, "gestalt pressure" (K. Lorenz); cf. p. 18: "Form".

> Arrangement as a positional relationship

> Symmetry as a positional relationship

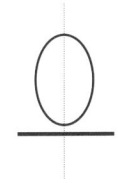

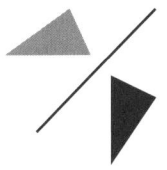

■ **Common features in terms of appearance**

As well as sharing position, things can also share their appearance, which is a second way of creating coherence. ■ **Formal** shared features are created by similarities of (outline) shape, size, height, proportion, quantity, direction of boundary lines (e.g. parallel) etc. ■ **Material** shared features are produced by similarities in material (e.g. surface structure) or colour characteristics (e.g. colour intensity, colour shade etc.).

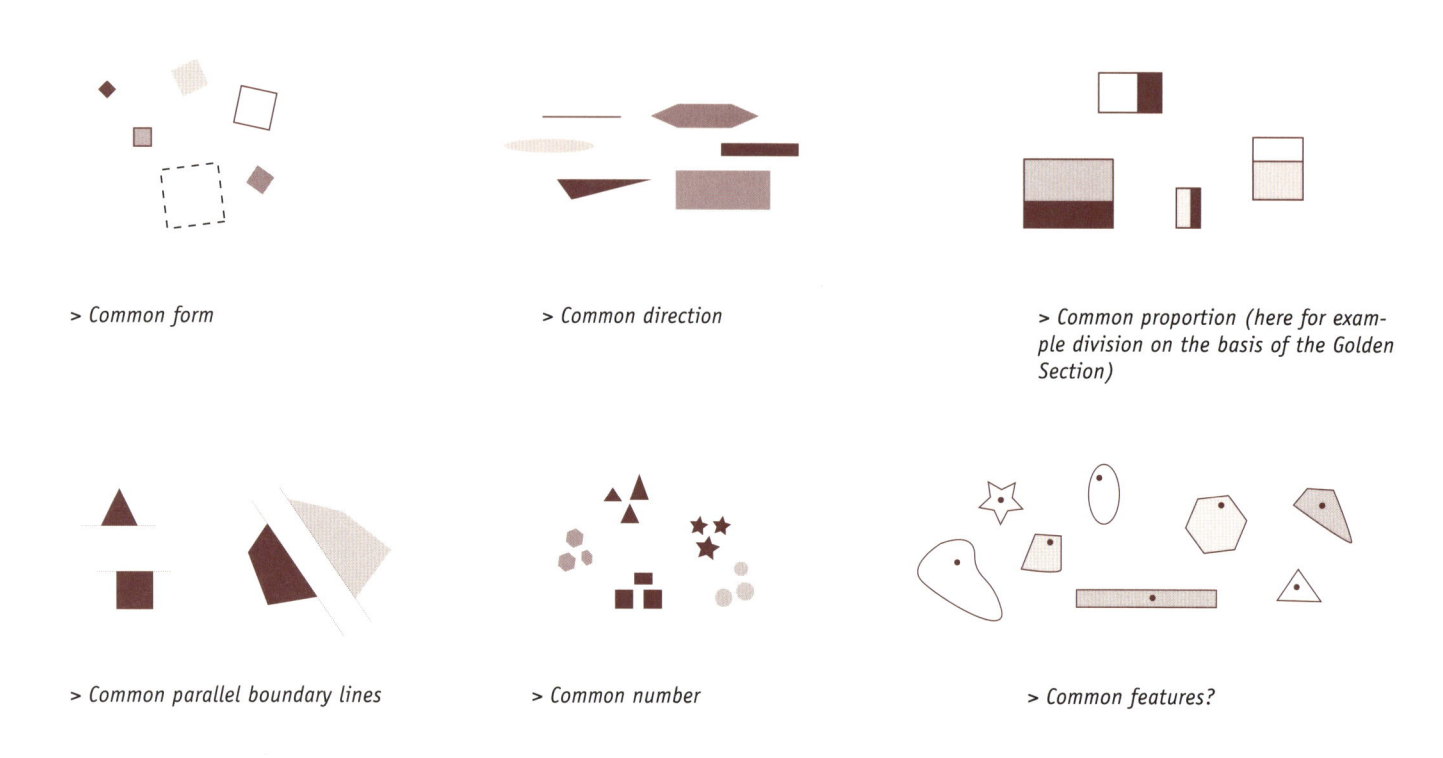

> *Common form*

> *Common direction*

> *Common proportion (here for example division on the basis of the Golden Section)*

> *Common parallel boundary lines*

> *Common number*

> *Common features?*

■ **Theoretical/thematic common features**

Coherence can also emerge independently of common positional or appearance features. We create theoretical/thematic unity by comparing things with previous (prior) experience, or by referring to conventions within our (cultural) existence, in other words to higher collective concepts whose theoretical/thematic "umbrella" can bring very heterogeneous things together. Theoretical/thematic common features can be relatively clearly separated (e.g. "cars", "plants", "benches". "animals" etc. [62], but less definite, immaterial contexts like "spring", "Tuscany". "light", "mourning", "time", "minimalism", "Asia", "Wittgenstein" etc. can also provide a link (the theme) between various things.

[62] Cf. also p. 20: "Form components", example "knife".

> A dog, a cockerel, a cow, . . .; or: mammals, birds, ungulates, . . .; or: animals

▬ Diversity

Uniformity requires common features, similarity, so that individual separate things can become components of a greater whole (a form, a gestalt). Here it doesn't matter what common characteristics are used to establish uniformity in a group of things; whether special positioning (e.g. closeness), formal/material or theoretical/thematic common features produce an effective connection: the only really important thing is that we find some common denominator as a basis for thinking things together, for making them into a unit.

This is particularly important for the design process: if a small number of common features is already enough to evoke unity (form, space), how does this matter in terms of the countless other possibilities for links between things?

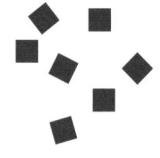

> *Uniformity by appearance (size, shape, colour) and position (closeness); diversity by arrangement*

> *Uniformity by appearance (colour) and position (linearity, symmetry); diversity by form and distance apart*

> *Uniformity by layout (square grid) and appearance (colour); diversity by form*

> *Uniformity by layout (closeness)*

> *Uniformity by layout (arrangement, circle)*

> *Uniformity?
. . . almost a circle (arrangement), certainly all people (theme)*

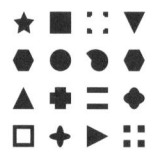

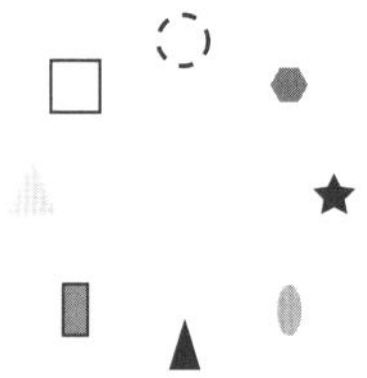

Uniformity always needs a certain degree of diversity if it is to be perceptible at all. This applies to every form of perception: without the contrast between quiet(er) and loud(er) we would not hear anything, without juxtaposing light(er) and dark(er) we would not see anything.

> Black cat on a full coal bucket

> White dove on fresh snow

Diversity reinforces the uniformity of individual form components. A large, flat area positively "needs" a vertical contrasting element to achieve its fascinating effect. The extraordinary spatial situation in a dense forest can only be experienced as a particular quality in contrast with a clearing.

> Flat area and tree

> Area and tree

> Clearing in a dense copse

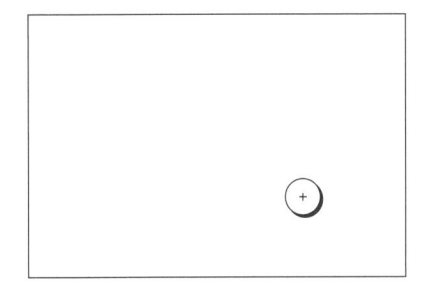

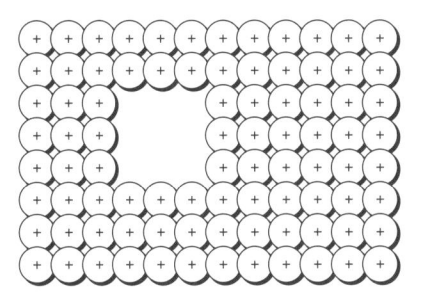

Diversity is the opposite of uniformity. Unlike uniformity, to which the individual components "subject" themselves for the sake of common qualities, become invisible, as it were, [63] diversity makes the particular nature, the special quality of individual things visible; it reinforces the "individuality" of form components, and at the same time makes the overall form richer (and more exciting).

[63] Cf. p. 18: "Superization", the human need to suppress the mass of individual pieces of information by superization; cf. also p. 55: "'Pure' space".

> "... it is like bald men who comb the last of their hair across their pate, which makes them look even balder."
>
> Wolf Haas, Silentium!

▬ Satisfying variety – the disturbance of uniformity

The diversity of design components is the basis for the variety of the design as a whole. Variety, along with uniformity, is the second fundamental quality of good design: the key to the quality of every design solution lies in the field of tension between uniformity (coherence) and variety (diversity). Unlike uniformity, which is created on the basis of common features (similarities), variety stands for differences within a design, for its ▬ multiplicity (formal/material) and/or ▬ complexity (theoretical). Variety "disturbs" uniformity, complementing it with the factors of diversity and ambiguity.

▬ **Multiplicity** means enlarging a solution in terms of space and things (e.g. with different materials, spatial sizes, form components, possible uses etc.). It is essential in (landscape architecture) design work that an object is not overloaded with components from the

outset [64]. This is also true above all because all the design components taken together represent only part of the actual, visible diversity of an open space in use: in fact additional diversity is "automatically" created by the users them- | *[64] Cf. p. 168: "Simplicity"*
selves (e.g. a mother pushing a pram, a fat man in a purple T-shirt, a kissing couple etc.) or by the traces they leave (trampled paths, worn benches, hearts carved into beeches etc.), but also by wear-and-tear/ageing of materials (weathering, corrosion, peeling paint etc.).

The fundamental truth is: the more diverse a design solution is in terms of certain design qualities (e.g. using different kinds of tree, path surfaces, directional links, spatial characters, areas of light/shade etc.), the simpler and more uniform the other qualities have to be (e.g. through common colour, position, height etc.) if coherence and uniformity are to be maintained.

_**Complexity** (ambiguity) means increasing the significance of the content of a solution and its connections through theoretical links and thematic references. Diversity may be a sign of quality that has to be used with care (too much diversity leads to lack of clarity, undue aesthetic demands on the users, too little scope for personal interpretations etc. and – ultimately – to the breakdown of form/coherence), but this scarcely applies to complexity: greater complexity (e.g. through linking ideas, references, quotations, allegories, metaphors etc.) fundamentally enhances [65] the quality of a design in the sense of significance-links (that are always there to be discovered) [66], without destroying "material" uniformity.

[65] *Unless extra diversity is also needed to make the complexity clearer, in other words a material "more".*
[66] *Cf. p. 159: "Stimulation/uncertainty".*

ideas

quotations

sketches

questions

additions

4.2 Characteristics of good design

Uniformity (resulting from common features) and variety (resulting from difference) form the basis of every good design. Many of the crucial qualities of good design are based on the dialogue between these two forces.

Stimulation/uncertainty

Tension

Weight/balance

Harmony

Connecting idea

Clarity

Simplicity

Stimulation/uncertainty

Phenomena that make connections and links clear very quickly are very much in tune with the human need to come to terms with our environment quickly: once we have recognized the connection, we "understand" [67] our consciousness is free to embark on new "connection adventures" [68].

In the creative discourse about design and the design process, all too clear connections are often seen as uninspired, boring or banal: lack of ambiguity in a design, anticipation of the search for connections is seen as an intellectual "spoilsport", leaving no room for the viewers' own interpretations to develop.

In contrast with this, phenomena that cannot be so rapidly placed in familiar contexts evoke greater interest, the urge to "understand" them. The period of mental uncertainty, of intensive demands on our consciousness before we understand, is important for the quality of design: the longer our consciousness "remains curious", the longer we feel that we have not (yet) discovered certain connections (but soon will be able to), the more lastingly we will experience and remember the connections that we finally "devise" (discover).

[67] "Understand" in the sense of classifiable, can be related to something familiar.
[68] Cf. p. 103: "Anticipatory orientation".

But if we search in vain for connections for too long, and cannot relate the phenomena that are occurring to something familiar, cannot "understand", then we lose interest and they are no use to us (any more).

The (design) development of good form is a constant tightrope walk between the two extremes "undue unity" and lack of understanding (incompatibility, decay), between clear links and incoherent individual phenomena, it means laying a trail and wiping it out at the same time.

So one "secret" of good, stimulating design lies in the tension between the (necessary) fulfilment of human expectations (quick understanding) and efforts to maintain the recipients' interest over long periods, to lay a trail for them so that they can discover unusual, new connections.

The "art" is in making the solution into a (solvable) riddle.

> *Unit or not (any more)*

> Unit

> linked by shape (outlines, parallel quality), content (colour, material quality), proximity and arrangement (symmetry)

> Linked by shape, proximity and arrangement (symmetry)

> Linked by content (material quality), proximity and arrangement (symmetry)

> Linked by form, content, proximity

> Linked by form and proximity

> Linked by proximity and arrangement (symmetry)

> Linked by proximity

> Linked by content, proximity and arrangement (45° symmetrical axis)

> Linked by proximity

> Weakly linked by content and relative proximity (in the context of this page)

> Only relative proximity; link can scarcely be made any more, objects tend to be perceived individually, separately

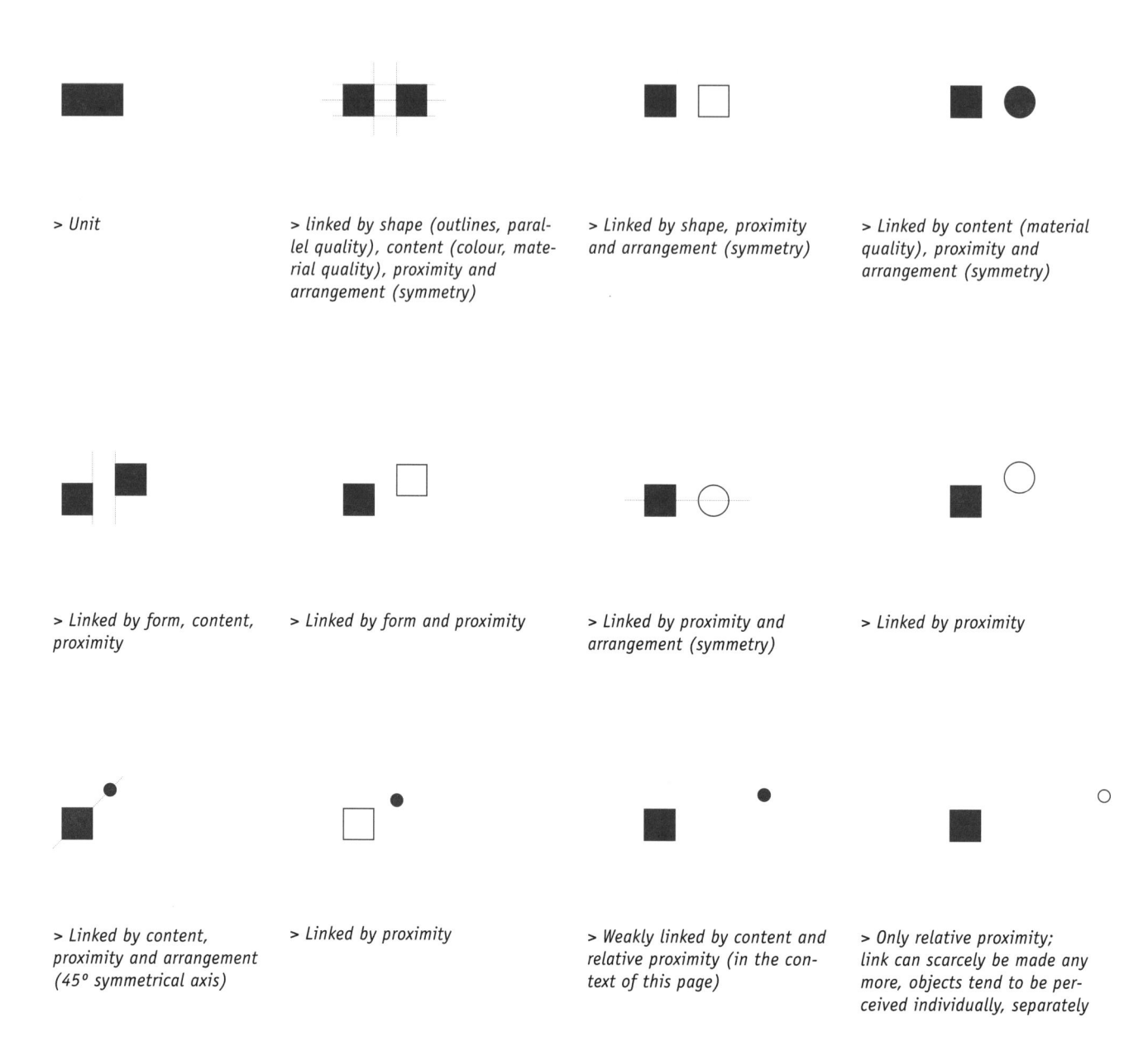

— **Tension**

Uniformity (as a measure of shared quality) and variety (as a measure of difference) are the key criteria for any good design: without variety a unit is insipid and uninspired, but without unity there are no reference points, pieces of evidence to enable us to create (discover) form. Uniformity and variety are opposite design poles, are thesis and antithesis, the "creation" and "destruction" of form.

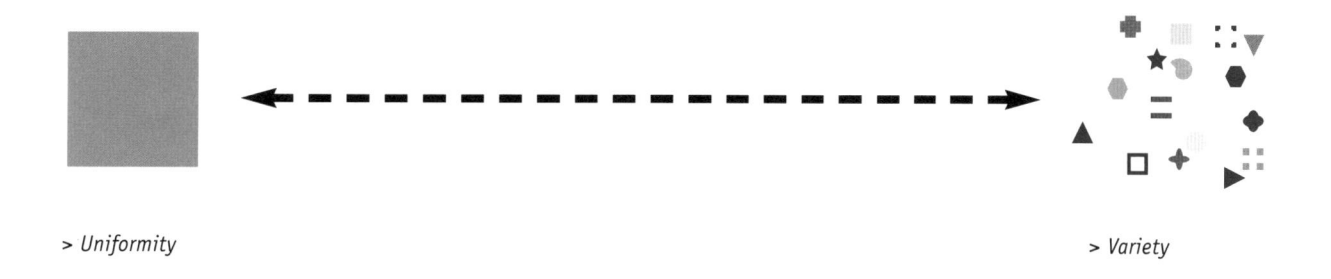

> Uniformity

> Variety

Variety attacks uniformity, enriches it, and indeed at its greatest extent so far that the unit's "bifurcation point" [69] is reached, in other words the point at which any more variety will "suddenly" destroy the coherence, the uniformity that combines individual design formal components to form different, unintended units [70] or makes them fall apart as a random mass of unrelated elements.

[69] Cf. p. 34: "Bifurcation"
[70] Cf. example p. 57

How much variety can uniformity stand?

How much uniformity does variety need?

As complementary elements, uniformity and variety occupy the end points of an imaginary line on which every "act" of design is positioned: within the design process and discourse, every decision about the appearance, position or theme of a design component (a bench, for example) will be examined to see how it behaves in terms of (the chance of) an overall design: does this

[71] Cf. also chap. "Creating focal points", p. 94 "Special position"

design component intend (for example if the bench is placed parallel to one of the edges of the building [71]) to support, reinforce the uniformity of the overall design (of a courtyard, for example), or will it weaken that uniformity, through diversity (e.g. an unusual, "self-important" bench), or enrich it through complexity (e.g. a bench that is at the same time a seat, a plaything and a tribute to Le Corbusier)?

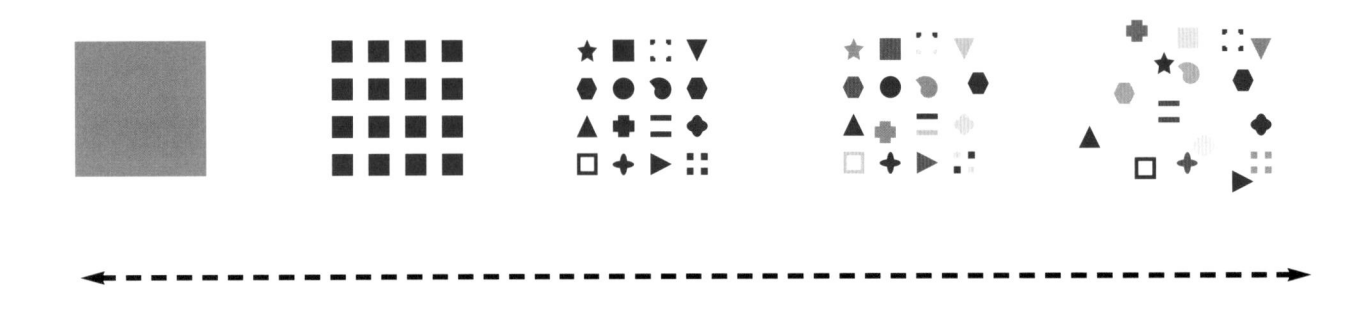

> Between uniformity and variety

The dialectical "struggle" between uniformity and variety is what makes form and design "exciting", "tension-inducing". Tension can be identified here as the strength, the power of the difference, it is the degree of resistance that design components put up against

[72] Cf. p.159 "stimulation/uncertainty".

the overall uniformity of a design. This tension is expressed in the viewers' heightened (inspiring) uncertainty [72].

The paradox of a good design solution:

More uniformity needs more variety.

▬ Weight/Balance

One crucial criterion for a good design is that of the (size) ratio of the different design components: ▬**weight.** Here we "weigh" in our minds the details that can be perceived, placing them on an imaginary scale. As well as spatial extent (large seems "heavier" than small), other qualities have a part to play here: colour (blue seems "heavier" than orange), colour intensity (red "heavier" than pink), brightness (dark "heavier" than light) but also the ratio of filled area to gaps (the larger the gaps, the "lighter" a group of things will seem).

▬**Balance** is the state of equilibrium between the different components of a design. We find balanced proportions calmer, less agitated than unbalanced ones.

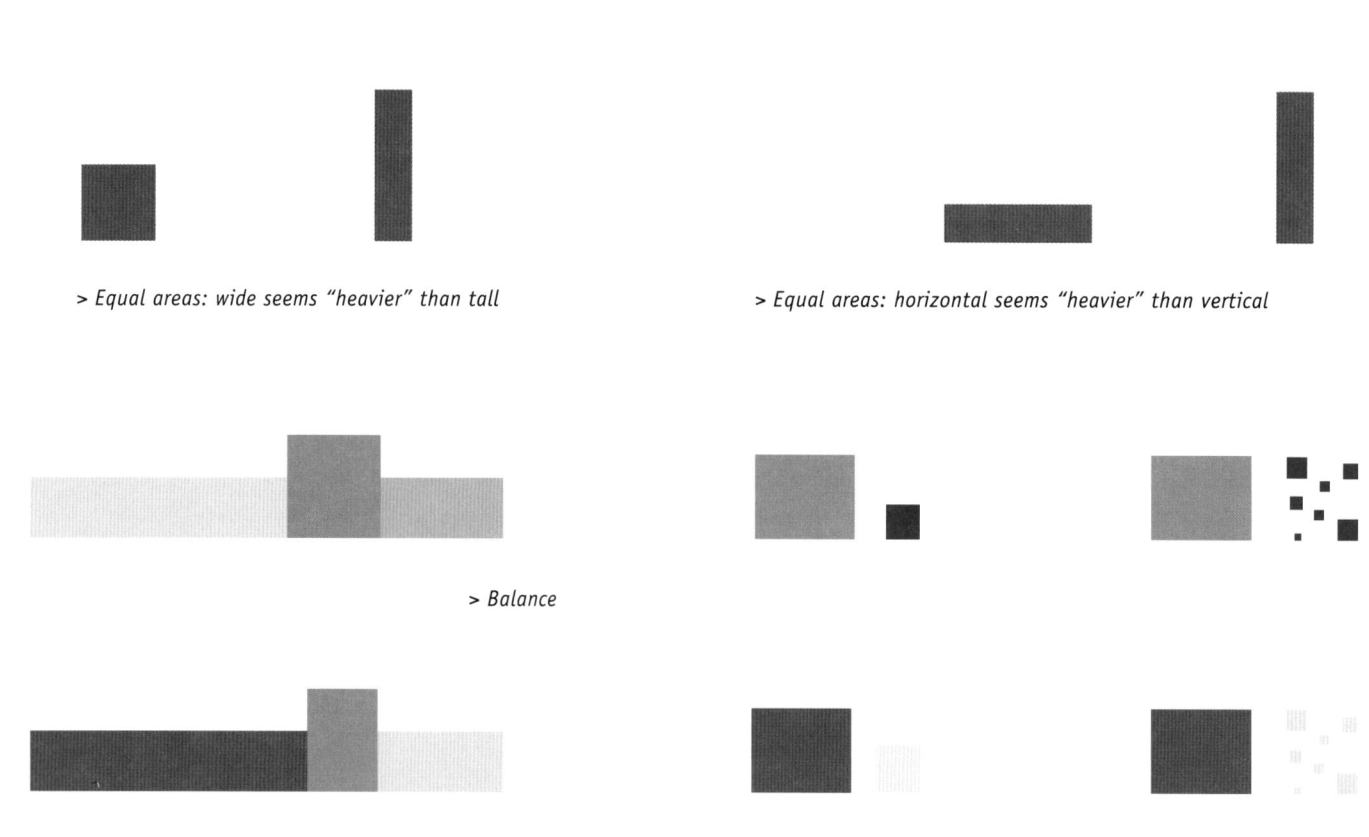

> *Equal areas: wide seems "heavier" than tall*

> *Equal areas: horizontal seems "heavier" than vertical*

> *Balance*

> *Imbalance*

Harmony

Colloquially, harmony must be one of the concepts that is most frequently called upon [73] to confer a verbal "quality blessing" on a design. Though it is usually (if it is thought about at all) confused with simple equilibrium, with relaxation and repose.

[73] The inflationary use of the concept "harmony" in design explanations is merely annoying in most cases. Classic example: "The new building fits in with the landscape harmoniously".

An attempt at clarification: in contrast with the **stable** equilibrium of calm, balanced states, harmony means moments of extremely **delicate** balance. Harmony is not a permanent state; in fact it is an extremely "fleeting" quality criterion that can be effective only through the simultaneous presence of two other supposedly complementary quality criteria: **stability** and **tension.**

"What is opposed comes together: the finest harmony derives from things at variance." Heraclitus

"Dissonance is the truth about harmony" Theodor W. Adorno

Harmonious states are moments of complete repose and simultaneous high tension, are moments of equilibrium against the background of an almost physically tangible collapse, are standing still and top speed at the same time: harmony is nervous repose.

The secret of harmonious moments lies in the fact that they make it possible to discern a certain state and its opposite at the same time and to the same extent.

Through design methods alone, harmony is a difficultly achievable (permanent) state: this applies particularly (though not exclusively) to landscape architecture; the mass of unpredictable, scarcely controllable factors that affect an open space at any given moment (people, weather, time of day, season, climate, smells etc. etc.) affect the imagined harmonious balance. So harmony in open spaces is a state that can be imagined (and is desirable in design terms), but as a rule can only be achieved for fleeting moments.

And yet:

Good design is the harmony of the complementary elements assimilated within it.

— Linking idea/theme/concept

Perhaps the most important characteristic of any good design is that of the linking idea, the concept, the over-arching theme, the "thread running through": the linking idea creates the theoretical/associative connection within the design solution, is the immanent controlling authority during the process during which it itself emerges, takes over the orientation and guidance function in relation to (as many as possible) design decisions that have to be taken; it is the rigorous guardian of uniformity. Good landscape architecture is always (also) a spatial/material interpretation, implementation of a theme, an idea [74].

[74] Cf. also p. 33: "Intention".

There are endless examples of linking ideas for landscape architecture projects: from horticultural show themes like "Yellow Garden", "Water Garden" etc. via thematic provisions of the kind that come from housing associations ("Please design a young people's park") or private clients ("My garden should remind me of my beloved homeland Corsica . . .") down to highly abstract themes ("Park of the Future", "Sequential Garden", "Heidegger meets Foucault") and many more.

An alternative to the design approach of the "linking idea", in other words working on the basis of a convincing overall concept, is the assumption that design problems can be solved by working systematically through a list of requirements or function lists. But experience shows that this approach is not very helpful in terms of "good" design. This is partly because one of the basic requirements for design, i.e. uniformity (coherence) can scarcely be developed or recognized from this approach; in fact it is almost bound to lead to a (barely comprehensible) conglomerate of incoherent individual elements (and not to formal components, to the parts of a whole). And the lack of an (intelligible, comprehensible) over-arching design concept makes it almost impossible for third parties to address the result constructively. [75]

[75] Cf. p. 31: "Intersubjectivity"; p. 159: "Stimulation/uncertainty".

There can be no (good) overall solution without a linking idea.

■ **Clarity**

The quality criteria "clarity" and "linking idea" are very closely related: given that our brain is always trying to classify phenomena as unambiguously as possible as they occur, clarity means rapidly understanding the relationship between an over-arching design concept (theme, idea) and its implementation as design (interpretation).

Important point here: clarity is not a synonym for simplicity (see below) or plainness; in fact it means – much more comprehensively

■ **reduction to essentials,** conveying a design idea lucidly.

Reduction is focusing – on essentials.

■ **Simplicity**

Simplicity as a mark of design quality means: fewer different design components, fewer formal and material differences, in other words less diversity, less "aisthetics" [76]. The age-old "less-is-more"-rule is still indispensable here. Simplicity, as reduction (and thus focusing) on "less", "automatically" enhances the significance of a form (-creating process); it makes the design idea more precise and reinforces it by focusing the formal components thematically and/or morphologically.

[76] In using the term "aisthetics" we are following an argument by W. Welsch, who detaches the term "aesthetics" from its "predominant restriction to art or even simply to the beautiful" and replaces it with the term "aisthetics (…) to address perceptions of all kinds, sensual as well as intellectual, everyday and sublime, worldly as well as artistic".
[77] Too much aesthetics, too much sensual stimulation, leads to a state of anaesthesia, lack of sensation (Welsch).

Beyond this, simplicity always works against inherent excessive aesthetic stimulation – an excess which does not just make it more difficult to look at essentials, but – in extreme cases – makes sensory perception per se impossible [77].

"If you have three things, choose just two. If you can take ten, then just take five. In that way you will be able to handle everything that you take more easily and surely."

Picasso on his way of making sculptures from found objects.

For landscape architecture in particular, simplicity is a fundamental, unavoidable quality criterion: open spaces are objects for "contemplation" only in exceptional cases, three-dimensional pictures (e.g. conservatories); in fact they are almost always built parameters, instructions for how to proceed and stimuli for (often very different) people. Realized and used open space therefore contains (we hope!) "automatically" a lively variety of human behaviour and traces to show that it has been happening.

Design simplicity is the key to lively diversity.

notes

ideas

quotations

sketches

questions

additions

4.3 Repetition as a tool

Design is coherence.

Coherence is achieved when position and appearance share common features, and similarities in terms of ideas and themes are given. Within the design process, shared appearance and position are derived from repeating material and formal characteristics or from positional similarities.

Thus coherence of individual objects is achieved and unity (design) emerges.

Repetition

Patterns

Grids

Variation

Transformation

Rhythm

Proportion

Symbols

▬ Repetition

Repetition means the **multiple use of similar things** [78]. It is a fundamental design tool (from fine art to music). It is always there to relate different things to each other, so that coherence, form (from the park to the sonnet) can emerge and can be grasped. Repetition as a design tool can be applied in a variety of different ways, obvious and subtle, concrete and abstract: it can relate to the material or colour qualities of things [79] or to positional relationships (e.g. a repetition of identical distances between objects) [80].

[78] Cf. p. 147: "Uniformity through common features".
[79] Cf. p. 150: "Common features in terms of appearance".
[80] Cf. p. 148: "Shared position".

> Prior experience through repetition

One of the countless differences between Aristotelian and Platonic thought is the explanation why people can recognize or name certain things: Plato worked on the basis that as well as a "fluid", changing world there was an empire of eternal, immutable "ideas", and that these were present in our consciousness, independent of sensory experience. And so according to Plato we recognize a tree without ever having been aware of a tree. Unlike Plato, Aristotle felt that sensory experience was the only key to understanding: he worked on the basis that we do not carry an object within us and accept it as a matter of course until it has impinged on our sensory perception: it is only multiple repetition of the same sensory experience ("trees") that leads to the "idea" of the tree.

Following Aristotle's argument, repetitions are also effective on the theoretical/thematic plane [81]. However, theoretical/thematic repetitions are clearly different from repetitions of appearance or position in their potential to be repetition tools as far as this chapter is concerned: repetitions of appearance or position directly (simultaneously) create three-dimensional form, but theoretical/thematic repetition is linked with prior experience – created by repeatedly seeing and recognizing – outside the particular design process.

[81] Cf. p. 150: "Common features".

In this sense, theoretical/thematic repetitions certainly are essential in terms of formal quality [82], but they cannot (unlike material/formal and positional repetitions) serve directly as working instructions, as (design) tools, as they have to "be there already" to create form/coherence.

[82] Cf. p. 17: "Coherence and prior experience".

The simplest kind of repetition is the **cumulative use of the same thing** in a regular arrangement or order. This kind of repetition creates absolutely clear, "loud" connections with a high degree of uniformity (e.g. an avenue, a formal grove, a military cemetery); the degree of difference is very small, the individual, form-generating component (e.g. the single tree, the tomb-stone etc.) becomes insignificant [83].

[83] Cf. p. 152: "Diversity".

\+ + + + + + + + + +

> Cumulative repetition of the same object in a regularly spaced row

> Repetition, linear (avenue)

> Repetition, grid (grove)

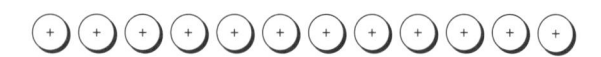

The fewer common characteristics are repeated, the less distinct the arrangement of the individual things is, the "weaker" the sense of uniformity becomes. But at the same time the overall form becomes richer, the individual form-gener- | *[84] Cf. p. 152: "Diversity".*
ating components are of a more striking presence, and become more important [84].

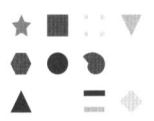

> *Repetition of only a few characteristics.*

> *Repetition of spacing [formally very different components but of similar (therefore repeated) size*

Design is repetition.

> *Structure*

Structure means the internal composition, the articulation of a formal unit: it defines its compositional qualities, describes the nature and form of ordering relations (e.g. hierarchies) between the different, form-generating elements of the whole.

Structure is a very basic concept and applies to all planes of design [85]: it describes the (structural) composition, following a certain inner logic, of a design and also the articulation instructions, the composition of individual components within an overall form (e.g. a lawn with individual groups of trees in a park).

[85] Cf. p. 14: "Order": structure as a definition of linear structures.

Structure is "invisible", an idea that has become a rule.

Patterns

Patterns are repeating or overlapping linear structures (areas are also characterized via the boundary lines) [86]. As form-generating tools they are the structural basis for creating coherence. In landscape architecture patterns are usually used as articulation instructions (structural background) for essentially two-dimensional ("ground plan-ish") contexts.

[86] Cf. p. 14: "Point-line-area-solid".

> *Basic pattern*

> *Filling (What could this be? Three-dimensional? Two-dimensional?)*

> Basic pattern

> Filling (What could this be? Three-dimensional? Two-dimensional?)

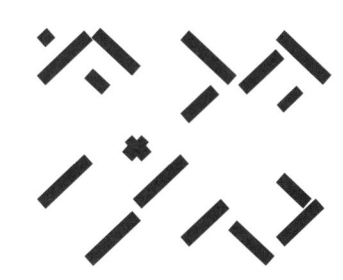

▬ Grids

Unlike patterns, which are usually more complex, **grids** are very simple (grille) structures. The simplicity of a grid's underlying pattern leads to very coherent structures. This means that things that are very different in themselves – with no thematic unity – can generate form. The clearest connections can be achieved with simple square or rectangular grids (some other geometrical forms are possible bases for grids, but they are less clear). The grid's actual potential for creating a clear connection between different elements by repeating the spacing becomes weaker the more complex its inner structure is (e.g. polygons).

Therefore: the more different the formal components are, the simpler and more regular the order of the basic grid should be.

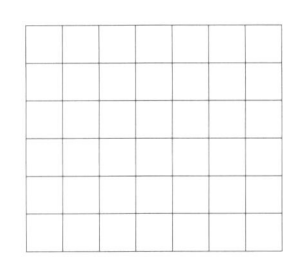

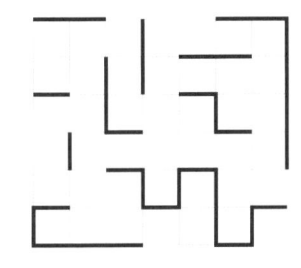

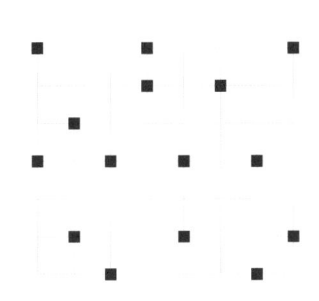

> Linear grid, square as a simple basic structure

> Possibility 1: occupying areas

> Possibility 2: occupying edges

> Possibility 3: occupying corners

> Point grid, rectangular

> Occupied grid with limited similarity (just similar size)

> Circular grid – difficult to read, needs similarity between the individual occupied points

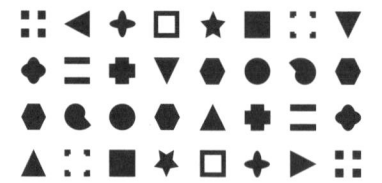

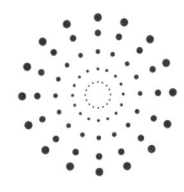

Grids are used at all stages of landscape architectonic superization: they can serve as a structural framework for the arrangement of formal components in a park, for ground coverings, for colour compositions inside flowerbeds and for many other issues.

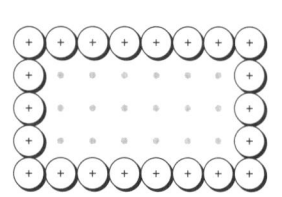

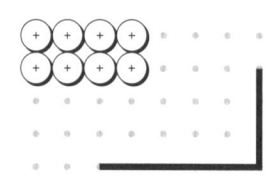

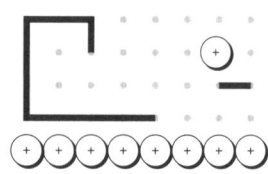

> Square grid

> Occupying a basic grid (What with? Trees? Space-generating walls?)

▬ Variation

Variations are repetitions of a formal theme by changing position and/or appearance. A basic form is always modified or interpreted in such a way that it continues to remain (more or less clearly [87]) recognizable despite looking different. Variations do not need a regular, directional sequence in order to create coherence.

[87] Cf. p. 159: "Stimulation/uncertainty".

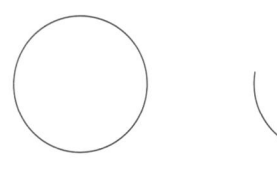

> *Variation – theme "circle"*

> *Variation – theme "death"*

■ Transformation

Transformations are series of variations that build on each other, and are thus directional: a basic form (an element, a shape) is **gradually** modified or interpreted in such a way that, unlike the variation, it is led in a particular direction, with a beginning and an end. The coherence of a transformation lies on the one hand in the common basic form (the basic theme) and on the other hand in the changing sequence of items building on each other, with each intermediate element being necessary to understand the change of form (though they do not all have to be present). The more distinct the final state of a transformation sequence is, the more important it becomes to show the intermediate stages, in order to make the connections comprehensible.

> *Transformation of a square*

_Sequences are transformations that change successively as a result of interventions that always remain the same, with each intermediate stage offered one after the other.

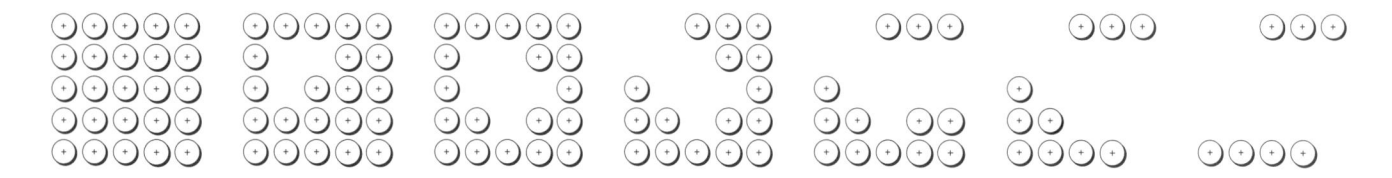

> *Sequence – a formal grove of trees is broken down regularly by leaving out a group of three each time*

> *Sequence – breaking down a row of trees (5, 4, 3, 2, 1)*

> *Sequence – breaking down a row of trees (4:1, 3:1, 2:1, 1:1)*

> *Height sequence within a group of trees (becomes clearer the more similar all the trees' other characteristics are)*

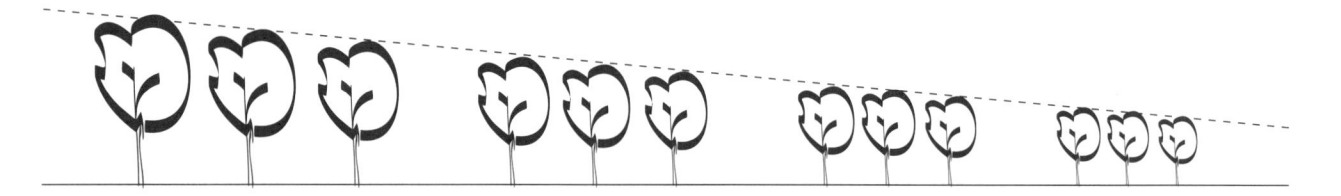

▬ Rhythm

Unlike sequence, rhythm repeats a characteristic combination over and over again. Rhythm is usually used to characterize linear relations that do not need a particular direction (otherwise sequence would be the appropriate tool) and where no clear (necessary) start or end point is needed (otherwise transformation would be the appropriate tool). In the three-dimensional arts (sculpture, landscape architecture, architecture etc.) rhythm can be experienced only as a series (in other words when the viewer moves), whereas in the time-driven arts (film, music), a time-based sequence is a given.

> *Rhythm – 3/2; 3/2; …*

> *Rhythm – plink, plunk, plinkplink, plunk; plink … (perhaps the trees are very different, then it gets jazzier …)*

▬ Proportion

Proportion identifies the precise (calculable) relationship between the pregnant measurements of things (e.g. the ratio of height to width), it describes the "subtle differences" in the way formal components relate to each other in terms of size. For example, if the same proportion is applied to many of the elements of an open space, this is a device that can be used subtly to create coherence "at a second glance".

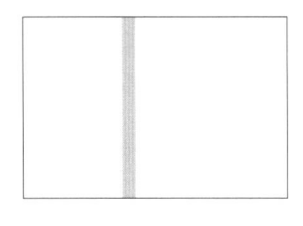

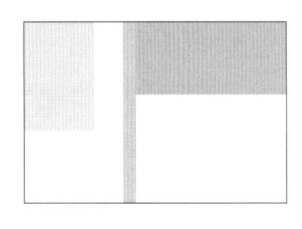

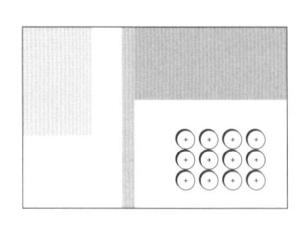

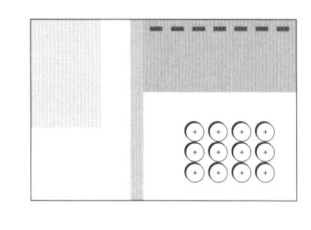

<1>   <2>   <3>   <4>

> Example: Plan of a rectangular plot. Ratio of borderlines 2:3. <1> Path cutting the plot in the same ratio. <2> Two further areas are introduced. The darker one is achieved by cutting the space right of the path in a ratio of 2:3. The borderlines of the lighter area have the same proportions, and also the grove of trees in <3>. The row of benches <4> has a rhythm of 3 (length of benches) to 2 (interstices). And so on (…and now the third dimension…)

> Scale

Scale relates to familiar size ratios between different things that are often visible alongside each other in the environment, in other words to the human ability to estimate the size of familiar things in relation to each other (e.g. dog and tree, locomotive and child etc.). The term "scale" presumably comes from presentation of information in plans: for example it would not be 'to scale' to draw a bench on a scale of 1:50 on a plan on a scale of 1:1200. Thus on the whole scale means using the right proportions within a certain context, a certain design identifying a size ratio between different formal components that is customary and familiar in terms of our prior experience.

> Out-of-scale pairs

▬ Symbols

Symbols (designs, allegories and quotations) are devices used for showing theoretical common factors [88]; they refer to something other (repeat this in terms of content). ▬**Symbols** are highly charged, meaningful signs that do not need a rationally understandable connection, in other words do not need an explanation in order to function. Symbols evoke certain connections in terms of mood or meaning, frequently they are archetypal memory images (e.g. colour symbolism, formal symbolism) etc.). In contrast with this, allegories and quotations need to be explained or the viewer has to be previously aware of them if they are to acquire meaning (be understood). ▬**Allegories** say something that is already familiar in a different way, they stand **for** something but without repeating this something formally/materially (problem: knowledge about this something is essential if the connection is to be recognized). ▬**Quotations** are fragments of a (very) familiar different form. In contrast with the allegory, which tends to be used on a theoretical plane, (architectural) quotations are used exclusively materially and/or formally.

[88] Cf. p. 150: "Theoretical/thematic common features".

notes

ideas

quotations

sketches

questions

additions

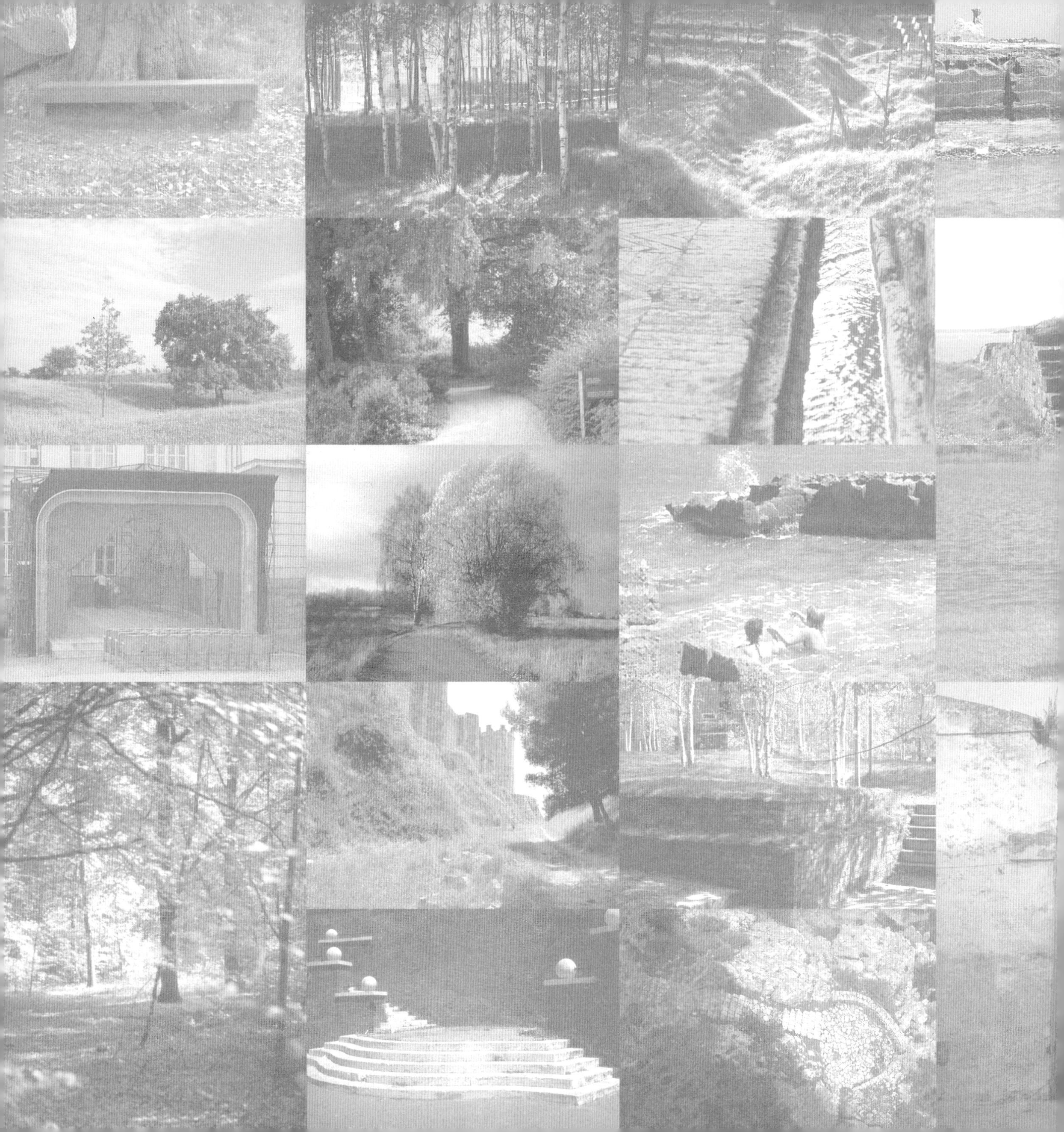

Verbotener Weg

Literature

Here is a true statement about design: it is quite impossible to produce a coherent pedigree and a full justification for the result (the design). In this case the result is a book, itself the result of a long design process, so logically the statement also applies. There have been too many influences, and there are too many obscure reasons why connections suddenly become clearer after conversations that can go on for hours, or after drafting a text. It is scarcely possible to reconstruct whether it was reading the paper, a sentence from Wittgenstein or a random chat with the baker's wife that "clinched" an insight.

But of course there are books that we found authoritative and vitally influential, others that people ought to know about, and others again that are simply stimulating and inspiring. Synthesis takes place in the mind.

Architektenkammer Berlin (publ.): "Experiment Freiraum", Schriftenreihe der AK Berlin, vol. 2, Sabine Konopka, Berlin 1991 ▪ Alexander, Ch.: "A pattern language", Oxford Univ. Press, New York 1977 ▪ Arnheim, R.: "Toward a Psychology of Art", University of California Press, Berkeley, Los Angeles 1966 ▪ Arnheim, R.: "Art and Visual Perception: A psychology of the creative eye", University of California Press, Berkeley 1969 ▪ Bachelard, G.: "The Poetics of Space", Beacon Press, Boston 1964 ▪ Barck, K., Gente, P., Paris, H. and Richter, S.: "Aisthesis – Wahrnehmung heute oder Perspektiven einer anderen Ästhetik", Reclam, Leipzig 1990 ▪ Bernstein, L.: "Leonard Bernstein's Young People's Concerts", Doubleday, New York 1990 ▪ Bocola, S: "Die Erfahrung des Ungewissen in der Kunst der Gegenwart", Waser, Zurich 1997 ▪ Bollnow, O.F.: "Mensch und Raum", Stuttgart 1980 ▪ de Bono, E.: "Lateral thinking", Ward Lock Educational, London 1970 ▪ Boullée, E. L.: "Architecture. Essay on Art", in: Rosenau, H. (publ.): "Boullée and Visionary Architecture", Academy Editions, London 1974 ▪ Cramer, F., Kaempfer, W.: "Die Natur der Schönheit", Insel, Frankfurt am Main 1992 ▪ Dethlefsen, T.: "Ödipus der Rätsellöser", Goldmann, Munich 2000 ▪ Feyerabend, P.: "Science in a Free Society", New Left Books, London 1978 ▪ Fischer, F.: "Der animale Weg", Artemis, Zurich 1972 ▪ Flusser, V.: "Writings", Univ. of Minnesota Press, Minneapolis, London 2002 ▪ Flusser, V.: "The Shape of Things", Reaktion Books, London 1999 ▪ Gaarder, J.: "Sophie's world", London 1995 ▪ Gamper, Ch.: "RaumBild", Diplomarbeit at the Inst. of Geography, Univ. Vienna, 1999 ▪ Gamper,

M.: "a place to be contained within corners", self-publ., London 2000 ▪ Grütter, J. K.: "Ästhetik der Architektur", W. Kohlhammer, Stuttgart 1987 ▪ Haase, R.: "Die harmonikalen Wurzeln der Musik", E. Lafite, Vienna 1969 ▪ Hackett, B.: "Planting Design", Oriel, London, 1979 ▪ Itten, J.: "Elemente der bildenden Kunst", Otto Maier, Ravensburg 1961 ▪ Kandinsky, W. "Vom Punkt zu Linie und Fläche", Bauhaus-Bücher no. 9, A. Langen, Munich 1926 ▪ Katz, D.: "Gestalt Psychology: its nature and significance", Ronald, New York 1950 ▪ Klee, P.: "The Thinking Eye", ed. Jürg Spiller, Overlook Press, Woodstock 1992 ▪ Koestler, A.: "Der göttliche Funke", Scherz, Bern 1966 ▪ Krier, R.: "Urban Space", Academy Editions, London 1979 ▪ Kunstforum International, vol. 145 "Künstler als Gärtner", 1999 ▪ Langer, S. K.: "Philosophy in a New Key: A Study in the Symbolism of Reason, Rite and Art", Harvard University Press, Cambridge 1957 ▪ Lorenz, K.: "Behind the mirror: A search for a natural history of human knowledge", Methuen, London 1977 ▪ Lynch, K.: "Site planning", MIT-Press, Cambridge 1962 ▪ Maturana, H.R. et al.: "The Tree of Knowledge. The Biological Roots of Human Understanding", Shambhala Publications, Boston 1992 ▪ McCloud, S.: "Understanding comics", HarperCollin Publishers, Inc., New York 1993 ▪ von Meiss, P.: "Elements of architecture: from form to place", Routledge, New York, London 1990 ▪ Metzger, W. "Gesetze des Sehens", Kramer, Frankfurt am Main, 1975 ▪ Plomin, K.: "Der vollendete Garten", Ulmer, Stuttgart 1977 ▪ Price, R.: "The complete droodles", Pocket Books, New York 1964 ▪ Prigogine, I.: "Vom Sein zum Werden", Lettre Internationale 45, 1999 ▪ Reichert, G.N.: "Proportion", Hochschule der Künste, Berlin 1987 ▪ Riedl, R.: "Die Spaltung des Weltbildes", Springer, Vienna 1985 ▪ Riedl, R.: "Strukturen der Komplexität", Springer, Vienna 2000 ▪ Schneider, M.: "Information über Gestalt", Bauwelt-Fundamente 44, 1975 ▪ Schwenk, T.: "Sensitive Chaos", Rudolph Steiner Press, London 1999 ▪ Serres, M.: "Les cinq sens", Grasset, Paris 1985 ▪ Singer, W.: "Der Beobachter im Gehirn. Essays zur Hirnforschung", Suhrkamp, Frankfurt am Main 2002 ▪ Smith, P.F.: "Architecture and the Human Dimension", George Godwin Ltd., London 1979 ▪ Stewart, I. and Golubitsky, M., "Fearful Symmetry: Is God a Geometer?", Blackwell, Oxford ▪ Valena, T.: "Beziehungen – Über den Ortsbezug in der Architektur", Ernst & Sohn, Berlin 1994 ▪ Vitruvius: "Ten books on architecture", translation by Ingrid D. Rowland, Cambridge University Press, New York 1999 ▪ Watzlawick, P.: "The Language of Change", Basic Books, New York 1978 ▪ Weischedel, W.: "Philosphische Hintertreppe", dtv, Munich 2001 ▪ Welsch, W.: "Ästhetisches Denken", Reclam, Stuttgart 1990 ▪ Wetzel, E.: "Stadtbaukunst", Krämer, Stuttgart 1970 ▪ Whitehead, A. N.: "Modes of Thought", Macmillan, New York 1938 ▪ Wittgenstein, L.: "Philosophical investigations", Blackwell, Cambridge Massachusets 1997 ▪ Wittkower, R.: "Architectural Principles in the Age of Humanism", London 1949 ▪ Wohlfart, G.: "Der philosophische Taoismus", Edition Chora, Köln 2001 ▪ Wohlfart, G.: "Das spielende Kind. Nietzsche: Postvorsokratiker und Vorpostmoderner", Die blaue Eule, Essen 1999.

Hans Loidl (*1944)

Studied in Vienna and Copenhagen. 1974-1986 free-lance landscape architecture practice in Vienna. 1976-1984 taught landscape architecture at the Hochschule für Angewandte Kunst, Vienna. From 1982 University Professor of Landscape Architecture at the Technische Universität Berlin, specializing in project planning and design. From 1984 landscape architecture studio in Berlin. Numerous realized projects, publications, expert reports, juries, lectures. Lives and works mainly in Berlin.

Stefan Bernard (*1969)

Studied in Venice, Vienna and Berlin. Free-lance work for various design practices (regional planning, architecture, landscape architecture, graphic design). Organizational work (exhibitions, workshops, lecture series) and various publications (book projects, contributions to specialist magazines). From 2001 partner in the b+m+s Landschaftsarchitekten practice, Berlin. Realized projects and competition successes. Also graphic work (books, exhibitions) and lectures. Lives and works in Berlin.

This book is also available in a German language edition.
(ISBN 3-7643-7012-2)

A CIP catalogue record for this book is available from the Library of Congress, Washington D.C., USA

Bibliographic information published by Die Deutsche Bibliothek
Die Deutsche Bibliothek lists this publication in the Deutsche
Nationalbibliografie; detailed bibliographic data is available in the
Internet at <http://dnb.ddb.de>.

Design: Stefan Bernard, Berlin
Translation from German: Michael Robinson, London
Production: Oliver Kleinschmidt, Berlin
Printing: Medialis, Berlin

This work is subject to copyright. All rights are reserved, whether the whole or part of the material is concerned, specifically the rights of translation, reprinting, re-use of illustrations, recitation, broadcasting, reproduction on microfilms or in other ways, and storage in data banks. For any kind of use, permission of the copyright owner must be obtained.

© 2003 Birkhäuser – Publishers for Architecture, P.O.Box 133, CH-4010 Basel, Switzerland
A member of the BertelsmannSpringer Publishing Group
Printed on acid-free paper produced from chlorine-free pulp. TCF ∞
Printed in Germany
ISBN 3-7643-7013-0

www.birkhauser.ch
9 8 7 6 5 4 3 2 1